Evelina

Evelina

A VICTORIAN HEROINE
IN VENICE

JUDITH HARRIS

*for Sally & Adrian
with love,*

Judy Harris

FONTHILL

Fonthill Media Language Policy

Fonthill Media publishes in the international English language market. One language edition is published worldwide. As there are minor differences in spelling and presentation, especially with regard to American English and British English, a policy is necessary to define which form of English to use. The Fonthill Policy is to use the form of English native to the author. Judith Harris was born and educated in the United States of America, and therefore American English has been adopted in this publication.

Fonthill Media Limited
Stroud House
Russell Street
Stroud
GL5 3 AN

Fonthill Media LLC
12 Sires Street
Charleston
SC 29403

www.fonthillmedia.com
office@fonthillmedia.com

First published in the United Kingdom
and the United States of America 2017

British Library Cataloguing in Publication Data:
A catalogue record for this book is available from the British Library

Typeset in 10.5pt on 13pt Sabon
Printed and bound in England

To the memory of Sir Ashley Clarke, chariman, Venice in Peril Fund,

descendant of the van Millingen family of Evelina.

CONTENTS

Widowed, childless, palaced, villaed, pictured, jewelled and modified by Venetian society

-- *Henry James*, on Evelina

1

The River

In the arc of Italian Alps soaring above Bolzano in early September of 1882, the sunlit days were as bucolic as ever in early autumn, and the wandering carvers who sold painted wooden toys from their backpacks still walked the mountain passes. Even when rains began, nothing seemed unusual, at least at the outset.

But then, in a bizarre twist, a ferocious snowfall swept down from the north. Drifts piled up in the mountains, and torrential rainstorms pelted the vast Po River flatlands below the Alpine arc.

Just as unexpectedly, the winds abruptly veered to the south, now searing the peaks with hot gusts. The deep snows melted, their runoff rushing downhill into the streams.

Trouble lay ahead for all the farms in the vast flatlands below. Among these was the Pisani estate near the mighty Adige River, which ran parallel to the Po and was Italy's second longest river. The huge estate was owned by the English woman known throughout the territory simply as "La Contessa"— Countess Evelina van Millingen Pisani, a commanding figure whose face at 51 years of age still revealed a remarkable beauty.

Two years before this, her Venetian husband, Count Almorò Pisani, had died, and Evelina had taken over the farm estate his family had owned for over two centuries. Almorò was a descendant of one of the most prestigious doges of Venice, and the estate, known as the Doge's Farm, lay at the hamlet of Vescovana, a half-mile north of the mighty Adige.

Beginning above Bolzano in the Alps, the Adige River rambles for 255 miles in a southeasterly direction all the way to the Adriatic Sea, to disgorge at Chioggia, a fishing town due south of Venice. In the meantime, it sliced through nearly 18,000 square miles of flat and often swampy river valley. In her time, her husband Almorò was still fighting to keep the wetlands drained, because the silt washed down from the mountains would often block the waterways and flood the farmland. The silt deposits made the valley in Evelina's day (and our own) among Italy's richest for agriculture; although the Italy of the late nineteenth century was literally dirt poor, there the fertile flatland produced abundant crops of maize, tobacco, and wheat, which were then loaded onto boats and borne downriver toward markets.

Ironically, the same silt-rich waters that nurtured the soil endangered the crops. The rivers were fairly shallow—in places scarcely nine feet deep—and so the waters easily surged over their borders to flood the fields. To protect them, the river banks had been conscientiously lined with concrete walls, some built 29 feet above land level (after all, the ancient Romans had invented cement that solidified under water). To protect the croplands near the Adige and its tributary, the Gorzone, which abutted Evelina's property, a honeycomb network of drainage canals had also been built, with sluice gates to give the farmers some control over the amount of water flowing through their fields and into the river.

The sluice gates were needed, for the floods of both rivers were notorious in history. So fierce was the flood in October of the year 589 that its waters wrenched away the entire vast ring of stone walls surrounding Verona, 44 miles from Evelina's estate, the Doge's Farm.

In this reclaimed swampland of the great valley, where once nothing but reeds had grown, a fundamental problem remained: that the big plantations which ran parallel to the Adige, like hers, lay a scant twelve feet above sea level. For the next 34 miles the river descended barely 25 feet.

Back in 1617, when what was now Evelina's property had just come into Pisani family hands, a land inventory showed "771 good fields, 777 fields that sink ... and 320 fields under water." Not long afterward, the Pisani were also warned that 431 of their fields were "subject to high water"—that same flooding which regularly afflicts Venice today.

The threat of floods did not diminish with time and technology. On May 23, 1856, Evelina's husband Almorò had been concerned enough to write his country manager, "Let us hope that the waters in the Gorzone River will recede ... "[1] But hope was not enough, and snow and ice storms did their damage with such nasty regularity that just two years later, after torrential winter storms, the farm manager wrote Almorò to lament that, "These repeated snowfalls and epochal ice storms have prevented us from doing a good deal of work here in the country. I hope the cold wave will do minimal damage to the garden."

During that peculiarly cold and hot early autumn of 1882, the danger of flooding was exacerbated by the fact that a goodly number of the slopes from the mountains to the north lay newly bare, because too many mountainside trees had been cut down for construction and for firewood. As a result, when that cruel mid-September of alternating snow storms and hot winds burst upon the land, the waters of the Adige rose swiftly, slicing through the river embankments in nine places. At the small riverside town of Grigno, flood waters smashed into the cemetery with such force that caskets were sucked from graves and their lids torn off, leaving a macabre vision of decayed bodies and skeletons floating downriver.[2]

Just as it had thirteen centuries before, the city of Romeo and Juliet became a principal victim in that peculiar autumn of 1882. Two-thirds of Verona was flooded as waters surged up to fifteen feet high. The town's great Ponte Nuovo bridge—the new bridge—was ripped from its piers, and two other bridges were destroyed. Twenty flour mills, whose wooden grinding wheels were turned by the river currents, were yanked from their moorings. Buildings already awash in the high water were smashed by debris spun downriver. Collapsing houses trapped families inside, and the bodies of the drowned were washed into the river, which had now turned a ghastly yellow.

At the outset, the dangers of the situation had been grievously underestimated. Later the *Almanacco Agrario* would lament defensively, "No one could have foreseen the misfortune which befell us, nor the truly extraordinary disaster, its gravity and extent, which has no comparison with any previous flooding. It caught us unaware and completely unprepared."[3] The news traveled far: the Italian consul in Manchester told John Davies Mereweather that nearly 200,000 were left homeless.[4] In their churches, English sympathizers collected money to help the victims. Back in Rome, 38-year-old King Umberto I ordered the army to intervene belatedly, and he himself would later pay a sympathy visit to Verona. In the end, this single event would cause 63,000 people to migrate from the Veneto, the majority to South America.

The floodwaters had not yet peaked at Vescovana, which lay downriver from Verona. Exactly as the *Almanacco* would record, those living on the riverside farming estates—including La Contessa—did not yet know the extent of the disaster that had just befallen their upriver neighbor, any more than they could know that the gigantic flood wave of the Adige was flowing southeast toward them at the rate of twelve miles per hour. From Verona, it would reach Vescovana in less than four hours.

Still, they knew enough to be concerned. Rain had been pelting down, day after day, for a week, and in the early evening of September 15, a handful of fearful farm proprietors and their peasant laborers converged on the banks of the Adige close to Vescovana to watch. Runoff canals bored through the fields to drain into the Adige, but, as the men watching saw, aghast, the rising river was forcing water backwards into the runoff canals. It was obvious that soon these would overflow and flood the fields, where the winter wheat crop had just been planted. Unless this overflow was somehow stopped, the crops would be ruined. What was to be done?

The most obvious solution was to open sluice gates everywhere, so as to spread the surge of canal overflow across as broad an area as possible. This would protect the farms at greatest risk—that is, those closest to the river.

Lying at a fair distance from the river, the Contessa's farm was less endangered than others. But to protect those farms closest to the river, in their opinion, "l'Inglese"—the Englishwoman, as they also called La Contessa—must open her sluice gates.

In the blackness of the rain-swept, moonless night, two of La Contessa's neighboring farm workers set off on horseback to demand her cooperation. For every eventuality, the men brought their guns.

When the two men racing on horses through torrential rainfall reached the gate to the Contessa's estate, they rang the big bell, which roused a servant, who in turn roused La Contessa. Wrapped in a great black cloak, she appeared in person at the gate to the estate. When the men demanded that she open her sluice gates immediately so as to diminish the flooding of their fields, La Contessa assumed an imperious pose.

"What?" she asked, eyes flashing. "And risk *my* wheat crop?" To her servant, she commanded: "Prepare my covered carriage and two horses. I shall handle this situation myself."

In truth, La Contessa was only partly English. Her father, Julius van Millingen, was a British citizen and a doctor. Although educated at the University of Edinburgh, for decades Dr. Julius van Millingen lived in Constantinople, where he was personal physician to the sultans and their families.

There he had met and married a pert, flirtatious young half-French woman named Marie Dejean, nicknamed Marionca, who had grown up in Constantinople. Married at just eighteen years of age, she bore Julius three children. Evelina was the eldest.

When she was six years old, Evelina was taken to Rome, to live with her English grandmother and a maiden aunt. Both were pious Catholics well introduced into Roman high society, composed of the scions of those old noble families who had supplied Catholicism with its popes and princes over the centuries.

In 1848, when Evelina was approaching eighteen, revolution swept Italy. Her father rushed to Rome to attempt to bring Evelina and the two brothers who were with her back to Constantinople. It took him a year, but in the end he succeeded, and for almost five formative years Evelina lived in Constantinople. Invited by a friend to visit Venice, she accepted. There she met Count Almorò Pisani III, the last descendant of the famous 18th century doge Alvise Pisani. Evelina and the Count were wed in 1853, when she was 22 and he was 38.

In 1880, 27 years after they were wed, the Count died at age 65, when Evelina was only 49. From that moment, Evelina made it her mission to improve the lot of the estate's 400 tenant farmers and to better the farm itself– its oxen and barns, chapel, and garden. Slowly, with newfound skills and dedication, this middle-aged socialite transformed what had been a run-down plantation into a model farm.

It was this farm, this life, which she was protecting that September night of 1882, when the flood waters put the plantation and all that she had built there at risk.

By the time the carriage carrying Evelina reached the banks of the River Adige, it was after midnight. Even in the dark, against the background of rushing, rising water, this former beauty wearing her long woolen cloak made an imposing figure.

The argument with the neighboring farmers over what was to be done continued until the first rays of dawn. At that point La Contessa flatly refused to open the sluice gates that would release waters onto her farm. "Why should the crops on *both* our farms be ruined?" she demanded imperiously.

By way of an answer, one of the men raised his gun and pointed it directly at her. His companion followed suit.

Evelina kept a loaded pistol at bedside, but that night she had come unarmed. Still, she evinced no fear of guns nor of men. She stared at them. "Go right ahead," she said haughtily. "Shoot me if you will."

The guns were lowered. Evelina turned away. The Vescovana sluice gates remained sealed, and the wheat crop was saved—her wheat crop was, at any rate. Elsewhere fields remained flooded for several months.

Historians say that Evelina then alerted the army, whose men built defenses which protected the fields.[5]

Still, at that dawn of tensions, Evelina could have been shot and killed. She was a thoroughbred, but she was also a woman alone, undefended, defenseless. She could have flinched. She could have meekly turned away, and perhaps she should have. If none of this happened, if this Victorian-era female product of Roman Catholic schooling, of Constantinople and Venice, was that bold, that able to confront disaster with the cool reasoning of a general, the reason lay not only in her past, but in that of her forebears.

This is the story of her life and its extraordinary times, and of their lives as well.

The Cosmopolitans

La Contessa was born in Constantinople on April 4, 1831, as Teresa Evelina Berengia van Millingen, and behind her indomitable will and self-possession were generations of prosperous, intelligent, and bold van Millingens. They, and she, were virtually bred to be cosmopolitans: she spoke at least four languages fluently; her father, Julius, spoke six, and could read ancient Greek and Latin as well.

Evelina's paternal great-grandfather Michael was Jewish. Around 1740, the young Michael quit his native Rotterdam to seek his fortune in the Dutch East Indies. Almost two decades later, he was in Batavia (today's Jakarta) and by then a wealthy diamond merchant, when French ships foundered off the Indonesian coast. Generously advancing money to the French admiral for their repair, he was repaid, and shortly afterwards migrated with his family to London, where they settled in Bloomsbury.

Michael's second son James, who would become Evelina's grandfather and hold an important role in her life, was born in Westminster in 1774 and was educated at the prestigious eleventh century Westminster School, near Westminster Abbey in London. There, a family friend, Clayton Mordaunt Cracherode, interested James in the study of numismatics, in what would become a lifetime obsession.

In 1790, diamond merchant Michael once again transferred the family, this time to Paris. Through a friend of his mother, sixteen-year-old James found work as a clerk in the banking house of a Monsieur de Van Nyver. Ever more intrigued by numismatics, James quit the bank to go to work for the French mint. His interest in contemporary coins led him to become fascinated with ancient coins as well, which over time developed into a passion for archaeology itself.

Young James had been working in the mint for less than two years when, in August of 1792, insurrectionists assailed the Tuileries Palace. As the violence increased, the royal family tried to escape, but were taken prisoner. That September, seeking safety, James's mother fled Paris for Calais, but his father had remained behind with James and his brothers. The Reign of Terror was only months away, and in that late autumn, James, not yet nineteen years old, was thrown into prison for no reason other than that he was a foreigner. For the next two years, he would pass from one Parisian prison to another before he was finally freed.

Despite that imprisonment, when he was at last released, James chose to remain in Paris for a time. The four years of the first French Republic—the Directoire—had begun in October of 1795. By that time James was sufficiently re-established, and he and his brothers spent several evenings in the presence of General Napoleon Bonaparte. In his diary one of James's brothers left a description of Napoleon, "a pale, sickly-looking man, with a sallow complexion." At mention of England, Napoleon would grow visibly impatient, the boy wrote.

His long lanky hair gave a still more cadaverous appearance to his countenance; but his eyes were dark and penetrating. ... He generally stood before the fire, and many of the visitors were grouped around him, and seemed to listen to him with peculiar interest.

But now James transferred to Calais, where his mother was still living. There he met and around 1797 married Elizabeth Penny, whose father, Christopher White, was also working in Calais. When James was offered work managing the Paris branch of an English bank owned by Sir Robert Smith, from Essex, he decided to return there. Smith, a member of the British Parliament, had been one of James's fellow prisoners during the Terror. Significantly for James's future interests, banker Smith was also a fellow of the Royal Society and of the Society of Antiquaries. With him to Paris, James took his wife and three young children, including baby Julius, who had been born in London on July 19, 1800; it was Julius who would become Evelina's father.

A few years later, the English bank where James worked in Paris failed. The family, by then expanded to four children, moved to Rome. The transfer was easy, for by 1809, Napoleon had made Rome into a province of France. French troops now occupied the Eternal City and had taken prisoner the pontiff, Pius VII.

James normally gave his acute asthma as his primary reason for transferring to Italy. In reality, the now unemployed Parisian banker had become fully aware that in Rome he would be able to turn his experience in numismatics, combined with his hobby of collecting ancient coins and medals, into a lucrative profession.

For a budding archaeologist with genuine experience of ancient coins and medals, Italy was the most important single source of supply, and James successfully cultivated his reputation as an expert and dealer in antiquities.

There was also ample demand: J. J. Winckelmann and Sir William Hamilton had spurred both the excavating of sites and the collecting of antiquities by the late eighteenth century Grand Tourists. In this, James would achieve remarkable success.

Typical of the dealers of his time, while selling coins, James also began writing learned tomes on numismatics, and from coins expanded into antiquities. Over time he became a specialist in the ancient Etruscan vases which he himself excavated near Tarquinia and Caeri (today's Cerveteri), north of Rome, and which he personally sold to important museums all over Europe. He joined various learned societies in London and Paris and attended their meetings, and in 1830, when he was 56, his book, *On the Late Discoveries of Ancient Monuments in Various Parts of Etruria*, was published.

In 1804, Napoleon's younger brother, Lucien Bonaparte, had come to live in Rome; later, Lucien too became interested in the rich archeological site at Vulci in Old Etruria. Theirs was a small world, and in his home in Rome, Lucien gave concerts attended by English expatriates. It would have been surprising had James not been among that small English circle.

Perhaps thanks to his contacts among antiquarians and coin collectors, the van Millingens were allowed to become tenants in the very grand Palazzo Odescalchi, one block from the Capitoline Hill, and originally designed by Bernini. In these palaces of Roman aristocrats, connections and social standing were criteria for choosing tenants. Then as now, their princely owners did not sell the dozens of apartments inside their palaces, but kept the palace for themselves and paid for its upkeep through rentals.

James's wife Elizabeth was a devout Catholic, who found her way skillfully into the society of Roman aristocrats as a lady-in-waiting to the Duchess of Lucca, Maria Luisa of Spain, the daughter of King Carlos IV of Spain and Maria Luisa of Parma, and hence a former Infanta of Spain. While still a girl of only thirteen, Maria Luisa had been given in marriage to a cousin, Luigi of Parma, who was made King of Etruria in Central Italy in 1801. Just two years later, when he was only 30 and Maria Luisa 21, her husband died of epilepsy. Coincidentally, Maria Luisa, along with the rest of the Spanish royal family, found herself in difficulty with Napoleon, whose troops occupied Rome, and was forced into exile. With the downfall of Napoleon, she was made sovereign over the Duchy of Lucca, a miniature state created in the post-Napoleonic year of 1815.

Most importantly for Elizabeth, her neighbor in Rome and fellow Catholic, the Duchess bestowed upon her the title of Contessa. Her social anointment as lady-in-waiting provided Elizabeth with entree into highest Roman Catholic society, with deep repercussions upon her husband and children as well.

Once the van Millingen children were in Rome, all were sent to study at strict Catholic schools. But when elementary school ended, young Julius was sent off to boarding school, first in the town of Foligno, in Umbria, and then, thanks to the intervention of his father, to Ealing, a preparatory school near London. From there Julius would go on to study medicine at the College of Surgeons in Edinburgh, from which he was graduated in 1821 at age 21.[2]

By then, his parents' marriage had failed. Elizabeth, ever more intensely Catholic, continued to move in the high church circles to which she had access through the Duchess. James, with his Anglo-Dutch background, had remained Protestant, and the couple's religious differences are usually given as the reason for their separation. Whether or not this was the real cause of their break-up, Elizabeth remained in Rome while James fled, to settle for a time in Naples before moving permanently to Florence. In this way, Julius, the boy who would become Evelina's father, grew up in a family conflicted by religion and yet conjoined by cultural sophistication and a cosmopolitan education and outlook.

In 1821, during his final year of study in Edinburgh, Julius fell desperately in love with a Miss Janet Robertson, who is described in van Millingen family papers as exceptionally "beautiful, clever and pious"—pious, Protestant, and, moreover, eleven years Julius's senior. But Julius was optimistic: planning to set out to India as a surgeon after graduation, he had high hopes that Elizabeth would accompany him there as his bride.

"My love for her is so great that I am determined if it be by any means practicable, to marry her just before I go out to India," he wrote his father, James, on August 29, 1820. Then he added: "Her connections are very good."

One of these connections was her brother, one of five, and a severe Scottish Presbyterian clergyman. Unfortunately for Julius, the beautiful Miss Robertson's Protestant pastor brother flatly forbade the marriage because of Julius's Catholic upbringing. To this prudish clergyman, it made no difference that Julius, influenced by the Scots among whom he had lived for three years while studying medicine, had followed his father's example and broken with his mother's faith to convert to Presbyterianism.

There would be no marriage, and her family's rejection left young Julius heartbroken. No train connected Callander, the hamlet where Janet lived, so Julius walked the 50 miles back to Edinburgh, while reciting from the book of prayers she had given him. From Edinburgh, he traveled on to London.

In London, the desolate Julius was introduced to members of a committee that had been formed to fight for Greek freedom from Ottoman oppression. The committee needed a doctor to attend wounded soldiers, so, casting aside his plans to migrate to India, Julius accepted their suggestion that he serve in the Greek cause for freedom from the abominable Turks. On August 27, 1823, he set sail for the isle of Corfu, supplied with surgical instruments and medicines provided by the Society of Friends (that is, the Quakers), and, in what would condition his life forever, an introduction to the committee's hero, George Gordon Lord Byron.

Byron, the champion of Greek freedom, was already in Greece at Cephalonia, an Adriatic coastal island. At about the time Julius landed at Corfu, Byron had fallen seriously ill, "seized with violent spasms in the stomach and liver." According to William Parry, an English sea captain in attendance at Cephalonia, Byron suffered convulsions that made the poet behave "like a maniac" until the medicine which was being forced upon him took effect. [3]

Byron's life until that time had hardly been salubrious. Only five years before this, he and his two mastiffs and two monkeys had been living in Venice between 1816 and 1819, mostly in Palazzo Mocenigo, a palatial home on the Grand Canal staffed by fourteen servants. In "Reviews of History" (a UK academic online magazine), Dr. David Laven of Nottingham University describes the life, or at least a major part of it, which Lord Byron had led in Venice:

> Not only did Byron spend most of his time in the city (when not writing self-obsessed letters or wonderful poetry) in a state of priapic drunkenness, but he quite clearly had next to no appreciation for its [Venice's] urban fabric, its paintings and its architecture, or even its inhabitants. Bar very occasional affectionate remarks about servants or sexual partners, Byron's letters are remarkable for his contempt for Venetians: the women were all 'whores' and even those with whom he had longer relationships were animalised—they became antelopes or tigers, referred to with about as much esteem as his dog Mutz.[4]

As we shall see, however, he had a long involvement with one: Teresa Guiccioli.

In the first week of September 1823, Byron sailed to a distant seaport village in the south of Cephalonia (Kefalonia, as it is also spelled) called Metaxata. With him were his dog Lyon and five horses; his novelist-adventurer friend Edward John Trelawny (1792–1881); the young Italian doctor Francesco Bruno and various other friends; plus the poet's personal valet, his steward, and five other servants. There Byron would remain four months. After only a few weeks most of his friends had moved on, however, and Byron found Metaxata excruciatingly boring: as he wrote to friends, it rained there incessantly, and he had few companions with whom it was worth spending time. "They [the Greeks] are such barbarians, that if I had the government of them, I would pave these very roads with them."[5]

"Here of course there are not many attractions," he wrote, "neither in the comforts of my house nor the melancholy view of the Black Mountain. There are no contacts with educated persons, nor are there any beautiful women." His best companion was his Newfoundland dog, Lyon. It was a last straw when a series of earthquake shocks rocked Metaxata October 5. Nevertheless, he remained there for four months.

In early November, Dr. Julius van Millingen, together with three Germans, descended upon Metaxata. "Impressed with the young doctor, Byron offer[ed] to employ him as a physician," relates the account in *The Byron Chronology—Scholarly Resources, Romantic Circles.*[6]

Was there more than being "impressed?" Lacking the availability of "beautiful women," it has been hypothesized that the relationship between Byron and the young Julius became, during the many weeks of tedium at Metaxata, something more than that of soldier-buddy or doctor-patient. Given his endless pursuit of women, some might find this surprising, but biographers of Byron speak of his sexual ambiguities, including during his Cambridge years. On this, Edwin van Millingen, one of the sons of Julius from his third marriage, confided to a friend that the poet and the tall, young, and broken-hearted doctor enjoyed a special sort of "comradeship" (Edwin's word). "Byron showed, as much affection for the young doctor as it was possible for a man of his extraordinary character to feel for another human being of the same sex."[7]

After enduring four dull months on the island, Byron seized upon a promising new adventure: Missolonghi. The city closest on the Greek mainland to Metaxata had been held by the Ottomans since 1770, but in May of 1821, its Greek citizenry had rebelled and had successfully ousted the Ottomans.

To this, the Turks responded by laying siege to Missolonghi. To their surprise, the people of Missolonghi resisted, and when the Ottoman siege failed, Greek patriots and their sympathizers seized upon Missolonghi, which they celebrated as the very symbol of Greek freedom. No one doubted that the Turks would launch another siege, but in the meantime the Missolonghi resistance had shown that the Greek cause could triumph and that an Ottoman defeat was possible.

Albeit no military man, Byron was as energized by this as he was bored by Metaxata. Flinging himself into plans to help the rebel army at Missolonghi, Byron set about raising funds from abroad, and donated 4,000 pounds of his own money to help transport arms to the heroic Missolonghi.

The plan was for Byron to leave Metaxata and the island in November of 1823 for Missolonghi. Bags were packed, boats hired—but then Byron was obliged to delay his departure. Young Julius the doctor was invited to join Byron, and on December 8 was sent ahead to Missolonghi, where he was to tend to the wounded of the Greek artillery corps.

On the day after Christmas, Byron, ever accompanied by the dog Lyon, finally set out for Missolonghi. Their voyage proved unexpectedly arduous. A supply boat accompanying them was captured and taken to Patras, and only freed January 4, ten days after their departure. As Byron and the separate supply ship moved into the port at Missolonghi at midnight, they were greeted by the Greek fleet stationed in the harbor with a 21-gun salute.

At Missolonghi, Byron found himself with 600 men at his command, but also personally responsible for paying for the food and wages for all but 100 of these soldiers. Byron also had to oversee arrangements for use of a printing press. He also formally appointed Julius "Surgeon in Chief of the Greek Forces," charged with setting up a field hospital.

Through it all the atmosphere was optimistic, for English ships were due to arrive under the command of that same Captain Parry who had attended Byron when he had fallen ill the previous autumn. From England, the captain was to deliver the money, munitions, and supplies which Byron had been anxiously awaiting.

On January 19, two weeks after Byron's arrival, ten Turkish ships were sighted. Terrorized, the Greek captains whose ships were in the harbor took flight. Wresting control of the port, the Turkish vessels set up a blockade. This meant that Captain Parry could not deliver the much-needed supplies from England.

For Byron, this spelled disaster. He had just turned 36 when, on January 22, 1824, he wrote a long and sorrowing poem which included these bitter quatrains:

My days are in the yellow leaf;
The flowers and fruits of Love are gone;
The worm—the canker, and the grief
Are mine alone!

                    If thou regrett'st thy youth, why live?
The land of honourable Death
Is here:—up to the Field, and give
Away thy breath!
Seek out—less often sought than found—
A Soldier's Grave, for thee the best;
Then look around, and choose thy Ground,
                    And take thy rest.

"And take thy rest." Worse was to come. Less than a week after writing those words, Byron learned that he personally was expected to furnish rations, not only for 400 of his own troops, but also for their families and livestock. In addition, the remnants of a decimated German corps had arrived to join the little army. In all, Byron was now responsible for provisions for 1,200 people plus a discreet number of horses.

But all was not war and trouble. Dr. Julius left a touching description of a child of nine, who became a favorite of Byron, for, as the poet said, she reminded him of his own daughter—that daughter, Ada, lost to him only a month after her birth, when her mother walked out on Byron. Julius has left an account of the plight of the Turkish child:

> The wife of Hussein Aga, one of the Turkish inhabitants of Missolonghi, came to me, and imploring my pity, begged me to allow her to remain under my roof, in order to shelter her from the brutality and cruelty of the Greeks. They had murdered all her relations, and two of her boys; and the marks remained on the angle of the wall, against which, a few weeks previously, they had dashed the brains of the youngest, only five years of age. A little girl, nine years old, remained to be the only companion of her misery. Like a timid lamb, she stood by her mother, naked and shivering, drawing closer and closer to her side. Her little hands were folded like a suppliant's; and her large beautiful eyes, so accustomed to see acts of horror and cruelty, looked at me now and then, hardly daring to implore pity. 'Take us,' said she, 'we will serve you, and be your slaves; or you will be responsible before God for whatever may happen to us.' I could not see so eloquent a picture of distress unmoved; and from that day I treated them as relatives.[8]

No less compassionate than Julius, Byron took the Turkish child under his wing.

On February 2, Captain Parry at last managed to avoid the blockade and to sail into port. Two weeks later, the two men were sipping cider when Byron's face suddenly became flushed and distorted, and his teeth were clenched. Staggering to his feet, Byron collapsed in Parry's arms with what were again described as convulsions.

The next morning, Byron, more or less recovered, dismissed the episode as merely a headache. Among those present was the Italian doctor Francesco Bruno, who, like Julius, was in his early 20s. Fresh from medical school, Bruno had accompanied Byron to Greece the previous summer. To relieve the poet's "headache," Bruno proposed applying leeches to Byron's temples. Byron accepted, and the subsequent bleeding went on for hours.

This conventional "therapeutic bloodletting," which dated back to Hippocrates and Galen, was known as "heroic medicine," and its aim was to rid the patient of those excess humors—and blood was considered a humor—which left the body unbalanced.

For a time it seemed to work, and Byron showed some improvement. But then he was weakened by what seemed a bad cold. Following this, during a meeting with Capt. Parry and other English naval officers, Byron was discussing creation of a new newspaper, the *Telegrafo Greco,* when he was suddenly racked by a convulsion which seemed to suggest an epileptic seizure. He took to his bed, but this time too he recovered.

The following week an earthquake shook the town of Missolonghi, as already at Metaxata. The quake is recorded by Byron in a line of the last poem he was to write, "Love and Death":

> The earthquake came, and rocked the quivering wall,
> And men and nature reeled as if with wine.
> Whom did I seek around the tottering hall?
> For thee. Whose safety first provide for? Thine.
>
> And when convulsive throes denied my breath
> The faintest utterance to my fading thought,
> To thee—to thee—e'en in the gasp of death
> My spirit turned, oh! oftener than it ought.

By mid-April Byron was himself quivering. He was feverish, vomiting, and had joint pains, chills, and a severe headache, as Dr. Bruno's journal records. Byron grew delirious, his hands shook, his pupils contracted. By that time, he had been ill on and off for at least six months. On April 13, young Dr. Bruno summoned Julius, who was by then all of 24, as a consultant. Julius diagnosed meningitis and prescribed more therapeutic bleeding. Dr. Bruno agreed to the cure, but this time Byron himself refused. At this, panic swept the little group crammed into Byron's room—friends, servants, the two doctors. Contemporary descriptions say that the room where Byron lay ill became a crowded babel, with Dr. Bruno speaking in Italian, others in Greek and English.

On the following day, Byron was again delirious. The two doctors huddled before agreeing upon the diagnosis, that Byron was suffering from rheumatic fever. They also agreed that bleeding continued to be the correct remedy.

Byron continued to refuse to be bled for another day. However, after he had coughed and vomited throughout the night, on the morning of April 15, he agreed to the therapy. Leeches were procured, and, according to Dr. Bruno's records, a "full pound" of blood was taken in the first bleeding, and another pound two hours later.

Once more Byron refused. Throughout the long night that followed, the town of Missolonghi was rocked by a violent storm that brought lashes of rain, lightning, and thunder. At that point, as Julius wrote in his *Memoirs on Greece*,

> I told him, that his pertinacious refusal to be bled had caused a precious opportunity to be lost; that a few hours of hope yet remained; but that unless he would submit immediately to be bled, neither Dr. Bruno nor myself could

answer for the consequences. He threw out his arm, and said, in the most angry tone, 'Come, you are, I see, a damned set of butchers. Take away as much blood as you will, but have done with it.'

The next morning, April 17, the leeches were again applied—though not to Byron's foot, for he said that "I will not allow anyone to see my lame foot."

But nothing helped, and at 6 p.m. on April 18, Byron whispered, "I want to sleep now," and slipped into a coma. Exactly 24 hours later, he was dead. It was Easter Monday, April 19, 1824. Byron was 37 years old.

Van Millingen family lore has it that Julius had encouraged ("inspired") Byron to write his last poem, which ends:

My days are in the yellow leaf;
The flowers and fruits of love are gone;
The worm, the canker, and the grief
Are mine alone.

Julius himself conducted the autopsy, diagnosing purulent meningitis as the cause of death.[9]

The news of Byron's death reached England "like an earthquake." The London *Morning Chronicle* synthesized English reaction: "Thus has perished, in the flower of his age, in the noblest of causes, one of the greatest poets England ever produced." When his body, which had been embalmed by a deeply mourning Julius, arrived in London, huge crowds turned out to view it as it lay in state for two days.

Within a few decades the 2,500-year history of bloodletting as therapy would be abandoned—but not just yet. That August of 1824, three months after Byron's death, Dr. Francesco Bruno wrote a letter to *The Examiner* in London in which he placed the blame for Byron's death squarely on the shoulders of Dr. Julius van Millingen. Bruno's argument was that Julius had delayed the bloodletting with leeches; the two also argued over where the leeches were to be applied.[10] Referring to himself in the third person, Bruno writes:

Mr. Van Millingen approved of the medicines previously prescribed by Dr. Bruno, and was not opposed to the opinion that bleeding was necessary; but he said to his Lordship [Byron] that it might be deferred till the next day. He held this language for three successive days, while the other physician [Bruno himself] every day threatened Lord Byron that he would die by his obstinacy if not allowing himself to be bled.

True, Bruno admitted, Byron had previously accused Bruno himself of the lowest of motives: a desire to be praised for saving Byron's life. However, wrote Bruno, still speaking of himself in the third person, as if to lend himself authority:

> Mr. Van Millingen, seeing that the prognostications which Dr. Bruno had made respecting Lord Byron's malady were more and more confirmed, urged the necessity of bleeding. ... The opening of the body discovered the brain in a state of the highest inflammation; and all the six physicians who were present at that opening were convinced that my Lord would have been saved by the bleeding which his physician Dr. Bruno [who is the author of this letter] had advised from the beginning with the most pressing urgency and the greatest firmness.[11]

In short, Bruno's defense was that not the bloodletting, but its delay, was the cause of Byron's death.

Seven years would pass before Julius offered his version of events in his 358-page book *Of the Affairs of Greece*, published in London in 1831. In it Julius claims that Byron had said he no longer desired to live: "'I have exhausted all the nectar contained in the cup of life: it is time to throw the dregs away,'" wrote Julius, quoting Byron.

Still, the shock of Byron's death and Dr. Bruno's accusations lingered, and for the rest of time Julius's reputation would be compromised as the murderer of the beloved poet. An obituary of Julius after his death at age 87, published in the London *Telegraph* Dec. 12, 1878, and reprinted in the *New York Times* a few days later, describes Julius as the "affable and communicative" doctor who had heard Byron "breathe his last sigh." Under the headline was a sly subhead insinuating blame: "Did His [Dr. Julius van Millingen's] Treatment Kill the Poet?"

Byron's life ended at Missolonghi, but Julius's was still beginning. Immediately following the poet's death, Julius contracted typhus. Upon recovering, he entered the Greek army as a surgeon and took part in several Greek campaigns against the Turks. In late February of 1825, less than two years after Byron died, Julius sailed with Greek patriots in an attempt to oust a formidable Ottoman armada that was laying siege to the island of Navarino (Neocastro). The fleet, Julius wrote, "consisted of eight frigates, twelve corvettes, 36 brigs and numerous transport-ships." Also on board were four disciplined regiments, each of 4,000 men, plus 2,000 cavalry and 1,000 artillerymen, he added.

The Greek fleet proved no match for this imposing force, led by the Egyptian Ibrahim Pasha.

At the same time, other ships under the orders of Ibrahim Pasha were laying siege to Missolonghi, that town which epitomized Greek heroism.

There, the siege lasted an entire year, or until the night of April 10, 1826, when starvation finally drove the Missolonghi from their homes. Missolonghi was lost to Greece, and many of the city's 10,500 inhabitants were massacred.

Ten months before this, Navarino had fallen to the Turks under Ibrahim Pasha, leading an Egyptian army. The Greek force in which Julius was serving as medical officer was obliged to surrender, and Julius was captured. On learning that his prisoner was an English doctor, Ibrahim Pasha made overtures to him, saying that he needed a physician: would Julius work for him? By Julius's own account of their conversation,

> Ibrahim, who happened then to have dismissed his private surgeon, a Greek named Gabrina, feeling the absolute want of another, requested Anastasius to inform me, that, on the Greeks surrendering the fortress, he would retain me in his service. Struck immediately with the embarrassing situation, in which I was placed by this determination of the pasha, and aware, that if I delayed any longer, my fate was inevitable, I formed the resolution of escaping by night with a Zantiot boat.[12]

The escape plan involved paying the crew $40 to help Julius, but it failed; according to Julius, the crew members did not trust him, and that night the boat was stealthily rowed away without Julius. His fate was sealed.

Ibrahim summoned Julius to ask if the Greeks had paid Julius for his medical services. Julius admitted that in theory he was to be paid, but that the Greeks were less than punctual. To this, Ibrahim Pasha replied: "If it is the case that you serve humanity, you may now remain with me. I am in need of a doctor. You will find me more punctual."

Julius has written that he again refused to work for the enemy of the Greeks. In his *Memoirs of the Affairs of Greece*, published in 1831, Julius revealed moreover that, after having been taken prisoner, he had chanced to meet an English naval officer named Captain Johnstone, commander of a British warship. Johnstone was on hand to ensure that the terms of surrender were met, and was decked out in a rather grand uniform in brutal contrast to the rags Julius was by then wearing. His first reaction on finding himself face to face with a fellow Englishman was "inexpressible joy" at this stroke of good fortune. As Julius later wrote in his *Memoirs*:

> As clearly as my agitation of mind would permit, I related to him the circumstances which brought me into the service of Greece; stated to him the embarrassing position in which I was placed [as a prisoner of Ibrahim Pasha] and from which he alone could rescue me. ... [I said I was] unwilling to remain with Ibrahim, who had now sent for me to let me again know his intention of retaining me in his service.

Julius was flatly rebuffed. Captain Johnstone cast "a contemptuous look" at Julius's shabby dress, and said: "Why, my good fellow, 'pon my word I am very sorry, I cannot do anything for you. You know you have forfeited every claim to British protection, by engaging in the Greek service. … Get out of the scrape the best you can."

At that point, "I felt myself entirely abandoned to the mercy of a barbarian," Julius wrote. In addition to the rejection by an arrogant English officer, Julius said that certain Germans who were already employed by Ibrahim warned him to beware of triggering the pasha's "savage" temper.

When Julius was hauled before him, the Pasha said tartly, "What business had you, young Englishman, to serve [men] fighting against their masters? … What wrong did you ever receive from Mussulmen [Muslims]?" He also argued that, as a medical man whose work was to aid humanity, Julius should continue to do so, in the service of the Pasha.

Even then Julius resisted, he claims, continuing to reject the offer to become personal physician to the Pasha. As a result, Julius remained a prisoner even though, as he wrote in his *Memoirs*, he did not overlook Ibrahim's relative generosity to the Greeks whose lives were spared. On the other hand, the Pasha accused Julius of ingratitude and warned him that he could easily have had Julius impaled.

On learning of his son's plight, his desperate father, the numismatist-turned-archaeologist James, appealed through the British ambassador to Constantinople, Stratford Canning, to have Julius released. Ambassador Canning obliged by writing the Foreign Office on Julius's behalf, saying that, "Dr. Van Millingen [is] a British subject who was pressed into the service of Ibrahim Pasha after the taking of Navarino." The Foreign Office was unimpressed. As Captain Johnstone had already indicated, nothing could be done on Julius's behalf, for Parliament refused protection of British subjects engaged in the service of a foreign nation. "The fact of his having been found in the service of the Greeks must preclude Mr. Canning from recommending his case," was the starchy Foreign Office reply of Sept. 8, 1825.

Fortunately for Julius, after he had been a prisoner for perhaps two years, Ambassador Canning managed to intervene, and successfully pressured Constantinople for Julius's release in November 1826. At that point, Julius might have chosen to return to London or to Italy, where his difficult mother, his estranged father, and a younger brother, Augustus, all lived.

But it was too late. Doubtless Julius was embittered because Captain Johnstone and the whole British Parliament had refused to bring him home, and had instead left him in an Ottoman prison. He may have seen advantages in exotic Constantinople, whose large and thriving international community would doubtless have room for a clever doctor.

For whatever reason, in 1827, he chose to remain in the Ottoman Empire. In the same way, his father James had elected to remain in Paris, despite having spent two years in a French prison.

In the meantime, the political situation was changing radically, for in a second Battle of Navarino the very year of Julius's release, British warships participating in the pro-Greek alliance along with Russia and France helped to decimate the Ottoman–Egyptian fleet. Following the victory in October of 1827, in which Britain participated, Julius's protector, Ambassador Canning, was suddenly forced to flee from Turkey.

Greek newspaper accounts, as reported in the English press, held that Julius had been a deserter. Nor could Julius have ignored the fact that Dr. Bruno had burned Julius's English bridges by publicly casting on him blame for the death of the romantic hero Byron. The shock waves of Byron's death resounded in Italy, too, where the poet had lived for six years, with long stays in Rome, Venice, and Pisa.

Indeed, a century later, Julius was still being blamed for Byron's death, as exhibited by Sir Harold Nicolson in *Byron, The Last Journey*, published in 1924 to honor the centenary of Byron's death. Nicolson's poisonous description of Julius's role in Byron's final illness concludes by saying that,

> Julius Van Millingen is not in any way a desirable person. ... He must figure with a certain unsavoury prominence in any record of the last adventure of Lord Byron, since he attended him in his illness, and in 1831 published a record of his [Byron's] doings and conversations, in which he bore much false, or at least exaggerated, witness.[13]

Worse still, Nicolson echoed the rumor that, rather than being captured by the Ottomans, as Julius claimed, in reality he had deserted to the Turks.

The fact remains that Dr. van Millingen entered the Turkish service, resided for over 50 years at Constantinople as physician to five successive Sultans, lingered on till the late seventies (1870s), a gaunt and sallow figure in his fez and stambouline, cut by the English colony, execrated by the Greeks, and pointed out to tourists as the man who had tended Lord Byron on his deathbed.

Nicolson's source for this was none other than Trelawny, who had been among those who assisted at Byron's death at Missolonghi, and had arranged his body's transport to England after its embalmment by Julius. According to an account by Julius's eldest son from marriage number three, James Robertson, or "J. R." (note that Julius had added to the name of this son that of his lost love, Miss Janet Robertson), Trelawny, believing that Julius was dead, had himself published in Greek newspapers articles attacking Julius. Thirty-four years after Byron's death, Trelawny would continue to heap coals on Julius's head in his book, *Recollections of the Last Days of Shelley and Byron*. Although late twentieth century biographers consider Trelawny given to "spinning yarns," in the words of literary historian David Hill Radcliffe of

Virginia Tech College, the book caused a sensation when published in 1858 and republished in 1878.[14]

Behind Trelawny's attacks, there appears to have been a nasty personal quarrel with Julius. In a section of his *Memoirs of the Affairs of Greece*, published in the *Literary Gazette* December 18, 1830, Julius had insinuated that Trelawny was gay (this ignored Trelawny's various marriages and affairs with women).[15] By way of response, Trelawny contradicted Julius's account of Byron's death, and in the same journal the following February wrote savagely that:

> I cursed Van Millingen and Bruno, as the two men, professing the art of medicine in attendance on Lord Byron, their victim, for their ignorance in not having pointed out to him the certain fate which would follow his tarrying in that pestiferous atmosphere against which, with his shattered and weak constitution, he could not hope to control.

It was now Trelawny insinuating that Julius was gay, via a vicious physical description that would be repeated a century later by Nicolson. In his article, Trelawny described Julius as a "tall, delicately-complexioned, rosy-cheeked, dandy boy, of simpering and affected manners ... who seemed to be under twenty years of age ... beardless, delicate and unpractised," a youth who whined and cried "like a sick girl" when speaking of his mother, a woman "who had taken the veil and was shut up in some Italian convent."[16] (As we shall see, this latter, at least, was false.)

Worse still for Julius's future reputation, Trelawny was also bruiting it about that Julius had agreed to work for the Ottoman Turks, not because he was their prisoner, but because they paid better than Europeans. Julius was treacherous, "base," a "branded liar," and a "mercenary" who had been provided medicines by the Quakers so as to give them free of charge to the needy, but had instead sold them. Julius was not even a proper Englishman:

> Of all sorts and conditions, all serving for pay and plunder, one man alone was mercenary enough to abandon the cause in which he was engaged, and for which he received pay, even to the deserter to the enemy, and that ... was Van Millingen, a self-styled Englishman. ...

At his father's request, the newly freed Julius elected to go first to Smyrna, with a detour to western Turkey to examine some antiquities at Kutahya, the city the ancient Greeks knew as Kotyaion, Latinized by their Roman successors to Cotyaeum. In Smyrna he had met pro-Greek revolutionaries, who adopted him as their family doctor, and in 1827 accompanied him on to Constantinople where, Canning now gone, Julius came under the protection of the Dutch ambassador.

That Julius became a physician in Constantinople is true, but he was not immediately and not only in the service of the sultanate. In letters published five years after Trelawny's book appeared, Julius wrote in the Istanbul daily *Levant Herald* on March 7, 1860, and the following day in the *British Star* (a Greek newspaper in London), that he had entered the sultan's service as "one of his Court physicians only in 1840, fourteen years after [having been] imprisoned by the Egyptian pasha and a full ten years from Greece's obtaining its independence." No connection existed between these events, Julius insisted.

A family memoir written by his eldest son from marriage number three, James Robertson ("J. R."), offers a personal account of Julius's doctoring in Constantinople. Julius was expected to tend to the serious illnesses like cholera, which struck frequently, and to take his turn for night shifts in the sultan's pharmacy. From his home in the mornings, he attended to the poor; in the afternoon he was to be available for palace duty.

What would those duties have entailed? Recent social histories say that, among other things, the sultanate required a palace physician to verify that the eunuchs of the sultanate were still just that, important because the eunuchs served as harem guards. And there may have been a few upper crust Islamic circumcision rites (*khitan*) as part of the palace medical services, because they were considered beyond the level of the more customary barber's knife.

In addition to practicing medicine, Julius once again emulated his father in Italy by cultivating a passion for archaeology. He eventually personally excavated the Temple of Jupiter Urius on the Bosphorus; he rediscovered Aczani, an ancient town in Phrygia; and he occasionally lectured on the subject, in Greek, to the foreign community.

Long before this, however, the impetuous, talented ex-prisoner Dr. Julius had fallen in love for the second time, or had at least fallen victim to passion. With no contact nor blessing from his father or mother, Julius was married in the Greek Orthodox church in Pera, in Constantinople, on June 22, 1830, at about the same time that he was penning his defense of his care for Byron.

His bride was a flirtatious teenager named Marie Dejean, who had grown up in Constantinople. Her French soldier father had fallen ill and died before she was born, and she was raised by her Greco-Armenian mother and grandmother. Ever known as Marionca, she was vivacious, pretty, and captivating, with dark hair and eyes. In her autobiography, published in 1882 in France, she offered a portrait of herself as an ebullient child.

From the age of eight years I made myself remarkable by my facility of learning and my high spirit. ... every day I knew my lessons better than did my young fellow pupils. At the same time I was so boisterous that I could not be kept in order against my will; so far did I carry my pranks that I would often come home with my dress all in rags, from climbing the very tallest of the trees in our garden.[17]

The high school she attended in Constantinople was French and run by a Madame Barbiani. One day, when Marionca was still a student there, she caught an eye infection and was sent home. Her mother summoned the eminent Julius van Millingen, physician to the sultan. "This gentleman was smitten by my charms to such an extent, that he did not hesitate to demand my hand in marriage after the third or fourth visit he had paid me," Marionca recalled. Not incidentally, Julius was presumably the first gentleman to have visited the girl, who was at most 17 years of age to Julius's 30. (In her biography written decades later, Marionca stated, slyly and incorrectly, that Julius was 20 years older than she.)

Initially their age difference did not pose a grave problem, but, along with her lively behavior, their diverse religions, and, as later became clear, her inexperience, did matter. To some extent it was for Julius a repetition of what had happened with Miss Janet in Edinburgh, but this time for opposite reasons. Raised as a Catholic in Rome, Julius had converted to the Presbyterian church while in Edinburgh. Marionca's account is that, "My mother accepted the [marriage] offer in the first instance." But then family friends, and especially the girl's Roman Catholic confessor, intervened, declaring that the girl, who was considered a Catholic, could not marry a Protestant. For the second time, Julius found himself denied the bride he desired because of his faith.

This time, the headstrong Julius would not take no for an answer. To the girl's home he sent an envoy, a "cunning" old woman, who dazzled Marionca with unspecified but "irresistible allurements." Marionca put up no resistance at any rate. Outfitted and made up to look like an old Turkish woman, before dawn the girl in disguise slipped out of the door of her house in the "native quarter" of Constantinople (her description) to meet her future husband at Bebek, several miles up the Bosphorus. In attendance nearby, arranged by Julius, were Greek Orthodox priests ready to celebrate the marriage, which took place on June 22, 1830. It would, in the end, lead Marionca, in her words, "upon that fatal course which must lead to perdition."

But not immediately. Although he had little time to tend to his girlish bride, within a month, Marionca was pregnant with Evelina. Still, in addition to following his patients in the sultanate, Julius found time to begin writing his version of Byron's death in an attempt to defend his personal position. His *Memoirs of the Affairs of Greece* appeared just six months after the wedding, when Marionca was five months pregnant.

The pregnant, young, half-European Marionca would have known nothing of the back story of Byron, Bruno, and Trelawny. Before her marriage,

Marionca had barely left her grandmother's house save to climb trees as a heedless child in the garden of her home, and then, as protection from the Muslim surroundings, to be accompanied by a maid to attend a Catholic day school for girls.

Suddenly her marriage left her off the leash. As she relates in her autobiography, in the solitude of her husband's vast, empty apartment—its furnishings were scant—in her hands Julius had placed a generous sum of money. She had never previously handled money, but now found herself pregnant and with money slipping through her fingers, with endless time on her hands. She was also more alone than ever in her short life and need answer to no one, or so she thought—no mother, no granny. To while away the months of pregnancy, she would lean out the window to hail passing peddlers, and from them buy all that struck her fancy: "linen, dresses, artificial flowers, carpets and a quantity of other things, for which I paid double or treble their value."

After one of these shopping sprees from her window, Julius inquired about the money he had given her. With gusto and no sense of shame, she explained that she had spent it to the last penny. The result, she recorded, was that her husband ran amok, overturning a table and heaving a dish at the head of the servant he blamed for having failed to keep Marionca under control.

Their marriage lasted less than seven years. But before it would lead to perdition—and it would—Marionca would bear Julius three children.

Evelina, born in Constantinople on April 4, 1831, was the first. Then came Frederick, born in 1833, and James, Marionca's youngest, born in 1836.

Pagan Pots and Holy Water

Her nearly seven years of marriage in Constantinople had left Marionca exhausted. Life there had long since become "most wretched," as she wrote many years later in her memoir, *Thirty Years in the Harem, or, the Autobiography of Melek-Hanum* (the name Marionca took after a second marriage). The essential problem was that her sophisticated doctor husband, Julius, had an ever more difficult personality, with hidden "monstrous" traits—her words. The sole bright moment in her life as a young bride, what made it bearable, was the freedom Julius gave her to "gratify my youthful caprices"—that is, to spend the money he earned tending to his patients, who included the sultan and his myriad family members, and the occasional favorite of the sultan living inside the harem.

The fact was that, while Julius may have gratified Marionca's "caprices," she was no longer youthful. By the time she was 25 years of age, Marionca was the mother of a brood of three. Her responsibilities to the children— Evelina, Frederick and James—were limited; tending them was the work of servants. This left her little to do but to daydream. She knew, or guessed, that life for the women in the harems of the sultan in Constantinople was far more pleasant than her own, and surely more agreeable than any outsider might imagine. It was whispered that the women in the harem amused themselves and enjoyed the luxurious living quarters set aside for them by the sultan. Together these fortunate women danced, they sang songs, they wore fine dresses. They gossiped.

Marionca could do none of this. She was not living in a harem; she was alone in a house with none but infants and the odd servant for companions. While remembering the happy days when she and her sister could climb trees in the garden of her mother's home, Marionca was left to wait in obligatory silent attendance upon her husband, whose medical duties kept him away ever more frequently. Her days were always the same: pregnancies, the bearing of a child every year or two, the nursing at the breast. Indeed, she was still nursing two-year-old James; as everyone knew, in this way she could postpone her next pregnancy, at least for a time.

Into this deep pool of tedium, it came as a bright ray of light when her husband suggested that Marionca take their two older children, Evelina, by then five-and-a-half years old, and little Frederick, age four, on a long visit to Europe. The point of the adventure was to explore the possibility of schools for the two older children. To attend to their needs, the maid, Caterina, would accompany them.

Marionca's heart leaped: when she and the older children left, two-year-old James would be handed over either to a wet nurse or weaned right away, for he was, in his father's plan, to remain at home with the other servants for the time being.

This shiny new chapter in Marionca's life, which Julius announced to her in September of 1836, was to begin with a winter season in Rome. There, as Julius assured Marionca, his devoted mother, the Countess Elizabeth—Betty to her friends—and his sister, Cornelia, would make Marionca and the children most welcome in their roomy apartment. As he explained to her, the apartment was in one of the most magnificent of princely palaces and was moreover situated in the heart of the Eternal City.

And there was more to tempt the restless young wife. Most conveniently, Julius's younger brother, Augustus, continued to reside near Rome, not far from his sister Cornelia and mother Elizabeth. After Marionca and the children had spent a pleasant winter season in Rome, this as yet unknown brother-in-law was to accompany them to Paris, home to Marionca's late father, where Augustus would help Marionca inquire into the possibilities for the children to be educated there. Giving this prospect further credence was that a female distant cousin of Julius who lived in Paris might be available as a possible nanny.

To the bored Marionca in boring Constantinople, the prospect of her first visit to Europe—the notion of spending a winter in a palace and then being unleashed upon Paris—loomed as "enchanting," as she wrote much later in her autobiography. To this zestful new beginning of her life Marionca looked forward with keen anticipation.

And yet, however alluring the prospect, try as she might (and she surely did try), in no way could Marionca envision what the future held in store for her and the children, for her horizon ended with the anthill scramble of crowded, narrow streets of Constantinople. Indeed it would be difficult for most of those who had never seen the Eternal City to imagine the magnificence of her future home. Little Evelina's English grandmother, who had been granted the Spanish title of "Countess" (we shall see why), resided in an apartment in the vast Palazzo Odescalchi, a grand palace which sat near the foot of two of the seven hills of Rome, the Quirinal and the Capitoline, abutting Trajan's Forum.

Dating from the fifteenth century, the Palazzo Odescalchi faced upon the elongated Piazza Santi Apostoli, on land which once lay within the enclosure of a large ancient Roman temple. This piazza and its magnificent palazzi encapsulated the unique history of papal Rome, and in the course of the three centuries before the van Millingens came to live there, the Odescalchi palace had been home to countless cardinals, some of whom became popes. Among the first owners were the Chigi, whose family pope was Martin V, elected in 1417. Passing into the hands of one of the very oldest of Roman families, the Colonna, the palazzo became the equivalent of a guest house, for the primary residence of the Colonna, which they and their ancestors had occupied since the year 1000, lay directly across the piazza, and was even larger than the Odescalchis, for from its core it had absorbed numerous neighboring buildings.

In 1622, the Colonna put their secondary palazzo—the one that would become Palazzo Odescalchi—up for sale. When a youth from Bologna in his 20s named Ludovico Ludovisi had the good fortune to have his uncle elected pope as Gregory XV, nephew Ludovico was made a cardinal exactly one day after that Gregory's election. With Ludovico's new red hat came wealth; not only would he shortly buy from the Colonnas the palazzo on Santi Apostoli, but the neo-Cardinal Ludovisi would also bankroll construction in Rome of the magnificent Jesuit Church of Sant'Ignazio, and also of the vast, rambling Palazzo Montecitorio, today home to the Italian Parliament. To begin improvements on his new palazzo, Ludovisi hired the already famous architect, Carlo Maderno.

When Cardinal Ludovisi died in 1632, the aristocratic Colonnas, who still occupied their stronghold across the piazza and adjacent to the Basilica, repurchased their old palazzo, only to resell it for 25,000 scudi to yet another important papal nephew, or *nipote* (hence our word nepotism), Flavio Chigi. Exactly like Ludovisi, young Chigi had most conveniently been made a cardinal following his uncle's election to pope as Alexander VII in 1655.

These Chigi were bankers from Siena, and initially Pope Alexander was a cautious spender. But it was not long before pontiff and family adapted to the Eternal City's Baroque lifestyle. Once again the palazzo was renovated, this time in the 1660s by Gian Lorenzo Bernini, already recognized as a great master architect. When completed, the palazzo facade was recognized as a masterpiece, with a huge inner courtyard elaborately adorned with niches to show off a host of white marble statues, vestiges of ancient Roman temples and theaters.

The palazzo remained unchanged until Prince Baldassarre Odescalchi purchased it in 1745. Their family pope had been Benedetto Odescalchi, elected in 1676 as Innocent XI. Across the piazza, the Colonna had begun an ambitious program of expansion; not to be outdone, Prince Odescalchi decided that his was too was small for a family of such importance.

On Odescalchi's behalf, two important architects, Luigi Vanvitelli and Nicolò Salvi, set to work, snapping up neighboring buildings until the palazzo had almost doubled in size. To mask the additions in this third reworking of the palace, they also doubled Bernini's harmonious Baroque facade, creating a second giant entryway. At that point the palazzo stretched down most of the side of the Piazza Santi Apostoli across from the basilica and from the Colonnas' palazzo. Not everyone was thrilled with the result: today's art historians call this an architectural hodgepodge which spoiled the graceful proportions of Bernini's design.

But never mind—Palazzo Odescalchi was still one of the symbols of Roman papal power, and when James, Elizabeth, and their children moved into it, still an Odescalchi property. Its owner was the Jesuit Cardinal Carlo Odescalchi, whose father, a duke, was said to have descended from one of the knights who had fought with the Emperor Charlemagne in the ninth century.

Besides its two great palazzi, the piazza which the van Millingens' apartment overlooked was extraordinary in other ways. The Byzantine core of its centerpiece, the Basilica of the Holy Apostles, dated from the sixth century. In this church the body of the dead Michelangelo Buonarotti had been laid to rest in February 1654. Shortly before dawn two days later, a farm cart drawn by two horses clattered into the piazza. Leaping down from the cart, its faux farmers—in fact, Florentine patriots—darted into the church, snatched Michelangelo's body from its bier and took it for burial to Florence.

Of her surroundings, it is a safe guess that Marionca's mother-in-law Elizabeth van Millingen knew little more than did Marionca, save for one telling fact: that living at the far end of their piazza (albeit in a smaller palazzo) was Henry Benedict Stuart, last surviving son of King James III and the Roman Catholic pretender to the British throne. Because of the English persecution of the Jacobite Catholics, Henry Stuart, brother to the more famous Bonnie Prince Charlie, had been born in exile in Rome in 1725 and had lived his entire life there.

Reputedly homosexual, Stuart was made a cardinal in 1747, then dean of the College of Cardinals. In 1751, he was also appointed Cardinal Priest of the Basilica of the Holy Apostles, next to his home and directly across the piazza from Palazzo Odescalchi.

By the time this last Catholic claimant to the English throne died in 1807 and was buried in the crypt beneath St. Peter's Basilica, the van Millingens had been living next door to him for at least five years.[2] Only a few steps from their doorway was the home of the late Henry Stuart and the Basilica in which he had worshipped and offered mass, both places redolent of a crucial chapter of English history. Although her official conversion to Catholicism took place around 1810, Elizabeth and daughter Cornelia, also a convert, would have attended daily mass in the basilica for several years before Henry died. The two could not have failed to see the elderly cardinal in the church— his church—and his carriage in what was their shared piazza.

In addition, that other cardinal who was their landlord in Palazzo Odescalchi had become Elizabeth's good friend, and was doubtlessly helpful in promoting her entry into Rome's most elite Catholic circles, and in arranging her introduction to Pope Pius VII himself.

For enter she did, becoming lady-in-waiting to the widowed Spanish Catholic duchess, Maria Luisa, the doyenne of Spanish Catholics in Rome. During the time when Napoleon's troops had occupied Italy, the widowed Maria Luisa had been imprisoned for four years in what have been described as harsh conditions inside a convent near the ancient Roman Forum. At the end of the Napoleonic era, Maria Luisa was freed, and the Congress of Vienna gratified her with what seemed to her a token gift, Lucca. There she spent summers only, but by 1823 had nevertheless founded seventeen new convents in and near Lucca. The rest of the year Maria Luisa resided in Rome, initially inside the Barberini Palace, and then in Palazzo Venezia, a few steps around the corner from Palazzo Odescalchi. (The mother of the Duchess's nemesis, Napoleon, had occupied a palace overlooking that same piazza, incidentally.)

It was there where her neo-Catholic lady-in-waiting Elizabeth served the Duchess as her companion for a decade or so, or until the Duchess died in Rome of cancer on March 13, 1824, at age 41.

Unlike his wife, Julius's father James, the scholarly antiquarian and neo-archaeologist, had no interest in the Vatican. His devotion was to the pagan antiquities that surrounded him, and provided him prestige and income. Among his special interests was the Etruscan civilization on the Tyrrhenian coast north of Rome. During their years together in Palazzo Odescalchi, Elizabeth's husband was often absent, digging for buried archaeological treasure in Etruria, publishing, and frequenting antiquarian societies all over Europe. As his knowledge and career progressed, he was also selling precious antiquities to museums in France and England, to such clients as the British Museum. He had private clients as well; one of these, Samuel Rogers, an English visitor to Rome, wrote of purchasing antique objects from James in 1814.[3]

The result was that the ever more Catholic Elizabeth and her husband James, ever more obstinately Protestant (and still presumably pro-French in sentiment despite the pontiff's being Napoleon's prisoner), grew ever further apart.

Their religious differences had long since driven a stake through the van Millingen marriage—or at least one of the stakes. Whatever other reasons may have been behind their separation, James eventually quit Palazzo Odescalchi altogether, to live first in Naples and then in Florence, leaving behind his wife and daughter. When Marionca and company were due to arrive, both his sons were already living independently. Julius was studying medicine in Edinburgh, and then briefly living in London. His younger brother, Augustus, had found work abroad with the East India Company, but, albeit fairly young, was already retired, and living in the Alban Hills southeast of Rome. Like their father, both young men by that time were resolutely Protestant.

Despite her husband's absence, in Rome, the neo-Countess Elizabeth was hardly alone. She enjoyed neighbors like her friend and landlord, the Cardinal. She attended the church of a Stuart. Her intimacy with the daughter of the Catholic King of Spain placed her within the exalted social circle of the upper hierarchy of the Church in Rome. Her intimacy with the Spanish royals was such that, after the death of the duchess, the Countess Elizabeth was granted a pension in recognition of services to her. Moreover, as Elizabeth would later confide to Marionca, she was also receiving a second pension from the pope himself, Gregory XVI, noted for the conservative and traditionalist views which she shared with him.

Popes, princes, palazzi, grace-and-favor pensions: this was Rome. The city whose atmosphere was a heady blend of holy water and pagan pots had already been a de facto home to two generations of van Millingens. With the arrival of Evelina and her brother, it would be home to a third.

Slowly the plans to travel from Constantinople to Rome and Palazzo Odescalchi took shape. From the port of Haydarpaşa, the four—Marionca, the two children, and the maid, Caterina—set sail on September 28 of 1836. They were among the few passengers aboard an English cargo ship, a cutter with a single mast (steamers would only shortly be employed on the route to Constantinople). Their first stop was at Ismir (Smyrna), where they were disappointed to find they were to wait in harbor, not for days, but for weeks.

Unfortunately, by the time they set sail for the second time, it was full autumn. Savage storms blew in, with such force of rough seas and high winds that the mast was wrenched off the ship. Waves slamming over the decks swept two sailors overboard to drown. Twenty-two days passed before they limped into port, at the island of Malta. By then Marionca and several other passengers were so seasick that they had to be removed from the ship on stretchers.

For another 25 long days, the ship lingered in the port at Malta. When it finally set sail for Italy, its first stop was nowhere near Rome, but 195 miles further north up the Tyrrhenian coast at Livorno (Leghorn to the English). But at last the quartet could leave the cutter to board one of the new steamships, which would carry them southerly, and finally fairly rapidly, down the Italian coast to the main Roman harbor at Civitavecchia. By the time they entered that harbor it was late January of 1837. Four months had passed since their departure from Constantinople.

Revealingly, in her account of this misadventure, Marionca never mentioned how her young children, Evelina and Frederick, reacted to living for sixteen weeks in a swaying boat. Nor did she mention Caterina, the maid.

But at last all four were in Rome, and all was well, at least at the outset. Grandmother Elizabeth welcomed with open arms Marionca, the children, and the maid.

"She was enchanted to see me," Marionca later recalled, speaking of her mother-in-law. She also noted that, although Elizabeth was approaching 60, her face still revealed traces of what must have been, in her youth, a certain beauty.

The four were also warmly welcomed by Julius's sister, Cornelia, a homely old maid, but friendly and obviously devoted to the van Millingen family. Indeed, it was usually Cornelia, rather than her mother, who wrote an "endless and often cloying set of letters, in both French and Italian," to keep brother Julius abreast of the children's progress.

Shortly after arriving, an apparently cordial and happy Marionca wrote, only slightly inaccurately:

> My mother-in-law was an Englishwoman, who had become a Catholic, and had been a lady of honour to the Duchess of Lucca. After leaving that court she established herself at Rome, where she assumed the title of countess.

Continuing rather slyly, Marionca added: "She told me that she had been very beautiful in her younger days." *She told me that she had been beautiful.*

Thus, the newcomers found themselves living in one of the world's grander neighborhoods, surrounded by churches that were gems of architecture and by reminders of the glorious history of Rome and of its aristocratic families and rulers of the church. If the details of architecture and history escaped the four from Constantinople, they could not fail to see, from the windows of their reception room in their palazzo, the elegant facade of the Basilica of the Holy Apostles.

Inevitably Elizabeth began to reveal her true thoughts. She would have grown particularly animated as she exclaimed to Marionca that, "Just think: Henry Stuart lived in the very building next door to ours. Henry, who preached in the church across the piazza, was the last." Here Elizabeth's voice would have saddened. "So unfortunate."

Unfamiliar with English history, Marionca could not have known what Henry was the last of; she could only have looked blank at this reference to the exiled Catholics whose claim to the English throne had died with Henry. Oblivious, Elizabeth would have continued, eager to impart more British lore. "And of course you know that Henry was terribly rich, but so as to help the pope during the French Revolution he gave all his money away. As Cardinal, Henry was the titular bishop of our very church, the Santi Apostoli."

Marionca had paid little heed to the old woman's babble, but at some point, she would have shivered at hearing Elizabeth say, "And that is where we shall all attend mass together—at the Basilica of the Holy Apostles."

This could only have been alarming to Marionca. Her background was Armenian Orthodox, and she had been married to Julius by Greek Orthodox priests. She knew full well that her husband Julius had long since turned his back on the Catholic faith of his childhood and, emulating his father James, had become a Presbyterian (albeit not Presbyterian enough to be accepted by the family of his beloved Miss Robertson).

The next difficult question after religion—but which was also about religion—was the children's schooling, important for Evelina who was almost six years old. Marionca was not interested in a Roman school, however, for her understanding of Julius's plan was that the four from Constantinople were to proceed in the springtime on to Paris—that Paris which had been her soldier father's home—to look into schools. Mentioning this to Elizabeth, she was surely given short shrift.

"Perhaps it is early for this to be decided," Elizabeth would have said crisply. "Let us just wait and see."

What Marionca did not know was that Grandmother Elizabeth had already made her own plans for the children. Before Marionca and the children had set sail for Constantinople, the countess had, in fact, written her son Julius on September 17, outlining a plan for Evelina's education, without bothering to inform Marionca. Elizabeth was not out of order in so doing: well before that date, Julius had made it clear to his mother and sister that he considered his wife incapable of educating his children, which was the whole point of dispatching them to Rome.

Taking charge, Elizabeth first arranged to have the two children baptized Catholics. Then, ignoring the plan for a transfer to England, she determined she would keep Evelina and Frederick permanently under her control in Rome, where they were to be raised as Catholics with a Catholic education. Having therefore made inquiries among her august friends in the church, Elizabeth was able to advise Julius that she had found a place for little Evelina at the French Catholic elementary school in Rome run by the *Dames Françaises*. In fact, in March 1837, two months after their arrival, Cornelia wrote to her brother Julius,

> We have sent Evelina to Mrs. De Casaun's school [the spelling is uncertain] to avoid her losing her time. We thought that, till the arrival of your answer, it would be well for her to be there; Frederick you should leave with us till he is of age to be sent to school.

The English Miss Fortescue, Julius's cousin, had been described as a possible nanny in Paris. But in the letter of March 1837, Cornelia says piously,

My father is well; he lately writes from Paris and says that Miss Fortescue's delicate state of health compels her to decline taking charge of Evelina's education. You see then that you must leave her [Evelina] here.

This too was a subterfuge, for a letter dated February 20 from Miss Fortescue reveals that Julius's distant cousin in Paris already knew that Julius expected his children to spend one year in Rome and then be transferred, not to Paris, but to England.

And indeed, in March, Julius himself wrote just this to Cornelia; Paris had never been more than a tempting morsel dangled before the ingenuous, hapless Marionca

Cornelia wrote again to her brother Julius on April 8. His children, she explained, and in particular Evelina, should remain in Rome, "not for one year, but till her education be finished."

There were other important secrets. As Marionca wrote much later, her husband had dispatched her to Rome in what was merely the first act of a wily plan, by which he was "determined to get rid of me as soon as possible."[4] By then she had realized that to his mother and sister Julius had confided his grave misgivings concerning his wife, which prejudiced them inevitably against Marionca before meeting her.

Julius had also failed to reveal to Marionca or to anyone in the van Millingen family, for that matter, the novelties of his personal life. The truth was that, having tired of his foolish young bride, Julius was already deep into an affair with a mature Greek woman, Saphiriza Kuladji, widow of a wealthy Greek butcher and the mother of two.

In Rome, Marionca knew nothing of this. On July 17, 1837, six months after her arrival, she addressed a fond letter of reproach to Julius for not writing her: "I think I have sent you seven or eight letters, it is inexcusable." She also mentioned needing money, for she planned to return home to Constantinople within the next six or seven weeks: "It is too long since I saw you, my dearly beloved Jules."

A month later, Cornelia wrote her brother reporting that cholera was sweeping Rome. "We are all well, and Eveline is at home. We are taking all precautions." While she was home, rather than boarding in the convent school, Evelina slept in Cornelia's bedroom. "She is studying well. Frederick is also well and always amusing, he keeps us all gay."

But then Cornelia struck another and slightly sinister note, advising Julius that, "Marionca is well, always thinking of leaving ... [and] desperate at not hearing from you."

Barely a month passed before a new letter from Cornelia was sent, giving details of how the two women planned to thwart Marionca's projected return to Constantinople. The letter dated September 30 reveals that Elizabeth and her daughter were now considering tucking Marionca away into a convent "for correction." However, at the moment this would be unwise, they had concluded, for to do so risked bringing dishonor unto the family. There could be no such step unless and until Marionca had done "some great thing," some truly horrendous act that would justify making her a virtual prisoner in a convent. This was not yet the case, Cornelia acknowledges. But in the meantime:

> I talked to her as a sister making her understand that the <u>only</u> thing for her to do was to accept <u>to remain here</u>, and to give you this proof of her obedience. ... You can be certain that I shall look after your wife; if she asks for a passport we will see that it is impossible. We watch everything, and if she does not fly out of the window she will not get away. ...
>
> She is bored here, but what can we do? We take her out driving as often as possible, but we cannot take her into society. ... We buy what is necessary for Marionca but she is not satisfied, and wants a month's allowance to spend. ... I see with winter coming she will need two warm dresses, and also [clothes for] the children; and if Marionca has a lot of money to hand she may find it easier to escape.

In this long letter Cornelia found time to mention Evelina too.

> Marionca says that Evelina seems stupid etc., but I assure you she is very sweet and talented. She is quiet and reflective, but as gay as is right for her age. ... In six months E[velina] had learned a lot, and it is better for her to stay there [in the convent boarding] as it is <u>better not to have her in the house with Marionca</u>.

At about that same time, Marionca again wrote her husband to say that the money she had requested from him had never arrived. Now, she specified, whatever funds her husband planned to send her and the children should go directly to Marionca herself; if sent to his mother and sister, she would never see a penny, she complained, not erroneously.

However unaware Marionca was of her husband's doings, she was otherwise observant and had by then pieced together a picture of the two women quite different from that seen initially. Her mother-in-law Elizabeth van Millingen (so recorded Marionca) was fond of luxury and well accustomed to a grand lifestyle, but despite having the benefit of two pensions, Elizabeth and her daughter Cornelia were living blithely beyond their means. Elizabeth was "crippled with debts, so that every day she was receiving a visit from some creditor or other, who demanded payment, sometimes not over civilly; a matter which seemed to give her little concern."[5]

The fact that Julius did not trouble himself to send money or even reply to all of Cornelia's letters had become of concern to the van Millingen women as well as to Marionca. It was obviously of no small aggravation to them that they were obliged to maintain financially the two children, the maid, and Marionca. On the other hand, this had the positive result of strengthening their hand against the despised Marionca, who was left with little recourse but to accept their willful ways and decisions about the children's religion and schooling. Marionca had no choice but to be kept a pariah, isolated and with no social life whatsoever.

Slowly Marionca, penniless and without a passport, also realized that Elizabeth, basing her ideas upon her extremely rigid and self-righteous version of Catholicism, was attempting to impose a religious education not only upon the children, but upon Marionca herself.

On the other hand, it is not difficult to imagine Elizabeth's inner rage, turned against Marionca, but also simmering against both her estranged aggressively Protestant husband in Florence and her errant son in Constantinople (the husband and son who themselves were not getting along). Her husband, James, flitting about Naples and Paris and London to attend archaeological meetings and digs in Tuscany, had abandoned his wife to her destiny, leaving her with insufficient funds to face down creditors.

And then her son Julius had humiliated her with the Byron business. Everyone in Rome's large and erudite English community—and she frequented a smart social circle of Actons, Talbots, and Eaglefields, among others—knew that Julius was responsible, at least in part, for the death of Lord Byron, and this had made his mother the butt of insensitive comments. It was fortunate that Elizabeth had attended the court of a Catholic Spanish duchess for a decade, where Byron's death mattered less, if at all. But after the death of the duchess, Elizabeth was again a woman alone—alone save for her daughter, the children, and the Church, against which her husband had turned his back. Similarly, her son, Julius, who renounced his Catholic faith to become a Presbyterian, was accused of being a traitor to the English by remaining at the sultan's court, electing to live in a world of Ottoman infidels.

Now both mother and son were conjoined in mutual longing to rid the household of Marionca, who was beyond reforming, and not worth it at any rate. Once the children were in school, Marionca became a dead weight and another household expense. The solution: to dispatch Marionca together with the maid, Caterina, to live with Augustus at Albano, southeast of Rome.

As Cornelia explained to Julius in a letter of February 24, 1838, "She [Marionca] had some months ago a fainting fit. She is in Albano, at Augustus' where she is content. She wanted to come here for the Carnival [the pre-Lenten party season] but it was impossible after all the unpleasant things that have happened."

Exiling Marionca to Albano was not a particularly happy solution, however, and not long afterward Cornelia again wrote her brother Julius in Constantinople. This time she was more forthright: "We have not seen Augustus for more than a month; he cannot leave Marionca alone, as he is obliged to have a sharp eye on her. Her conduct here was so bad ... "

Increasingly, Cornelia's tone took a despairing turn. Writing April 21, still unaware that he had a new relationship in Constantinople, she complained at her brother's seeming indifference:

> My dear Julius, In truth your silence gives us cause for great sorrow, more than I can say. No answer to our letters of 27th February, not a word from you since last September, and without news that I get from time to time from the good 'Stiminian' priest I might think you dead. I cannot think how you excuse yourself this fault towards mother and sister. ... The least you can do is to keep in touch with what is happening to your wife, who is the cross of our family. Poor mad creature.

Each letter revealed Marionca plunging ever deeper toward disaster. The "poor mad creature" was now terrorizing Julius's younger brother Augustus in Albano, Cornelia admitted. The maid, Caterina, was also frightened, for Marionca had allegedly threatened to kill her. Augustus's own life was "in danger," but nevertheless it was impossible to rid him of Marionca, because not even a convent will have "such a dangerous person," as Cornelia wrote.

In Albano, moreover, Marionca had taken three lovers "of the lowest class." On a night when Augustus was away, one of these men slept in his house. Hearing a noise, the maid discovered him—and was physically attacked by Marionca. So, concludes Cornelia, "I am going to <u>send her back to you</u>" [Cornelia's underscoring].

Cornelia went on to explain that, when the children, in the care of Marionca and the maid, were visiting in Livorno (Leghorn), on the coast near Pisa, "a Polish gentleman" tried to seize Evelina and bear the child away. Fortunately, Caterina had saved Evelina, Cornelia wrote, adding that she had also learned that, during the time Marionca was still living in their flat inside the Palazzo Odescalchi in Rome, she had opened a window so as to allow a gentleman caller to climb inside. Marionca had moreover tried to set fire to the house and to rob Elizabeth and Cornelia: "My maid saw her on the night before, she ran through all the rooms with a light [candle] in her hands. As she was quite naked, my maid was afraid she had become mad as a consequence of her illness."

Marionca letting a man into his mother's home, a naked Marionca racing about the flat in Palazzo Odescalchi with a lighted candle: however deeply in love with the butcher's widow, Julius must have reeled from news like this— reeled, but not in fact reacted. His silence continued.

Marionca has written her own version. Her situation was "a real hell on earth, in which I was subjected to the most cruel refinements of martyrdom," both when tucked away in Albano with Augustus, and when alone in Rome with the two small children and with the irreproachable but evil mother-in-law, who spent most of the day in church. Elizabeth had forced her into "strict retirement," Marionca wrote, "a dungeon, in which my mother-in-law had given loose to numberless intrigues and cabals ... [I was] the victim of a vile treachery." It was their persecution of her which had brought Marionca to the point of a nervous breakdown.

> The countess, who was anxious to secure the favour of the Pope, hurried me from Rome, and gave my children, Evelyn and Frederick, into the hands of the priests. Then the countess and her son used every exertion, the one to secure her prey, the other to satisfy public opinion; between them my poor children's affections were distracted, were torn to pieces and ruined for ever.
>
> [Julius] only wanted a pretext for getting a divorce, and marrying another woman. The countess, therefore, came to his aid, and by dint of moral and physical tortures she succeeded in bringing upon me an attack of madness. Scarcely had the symptoms manifested themselves than she wrote to her son, the doctor, who hastened to the Greek Patriarchate at Constantinople to demand a divorce.[6]

If Marionca's version was that she was driven into a nervous breakdown, her husband's was that her depraved conduct justified his actions. "She resisted all advice to return to a life of virtue," was the version Julius wrote much later, in a pamphlet dated Oct. 22, 1842.[7]

Not surprisingly, Augustus now appealed to his brother to take Marionca back to Constantinople, but Julius refused to have her, suggesting in cavalier fashion that she be kept in Rome, perhaps in a convent. Finally, Augustus could take no more of her. At the end of his tether, he dispatched Marionca from Albano to Florence and into the custody of Julius's father, the stern Protestant numismatist-cum-archaeologist, James.

Back in Constantinople, Julius successfully sued for divorce from Marionca, granted on June 22, 1838, by a Greek ecclesiastical court without benefit of witnesses or testimony from his wife, who knew nothing about it at the time.

In Florence, still with Marionca, James, who was also unaware of his son's divorce, had wearied of the whole business, and offered to pay for Marionca to return to Turkey—although not, he specified, to Constantinople, but to Smyrna.

Marionca accepted his offer. On July 4, 1838, sixteen months after her arrival in Italy, she left Florence, but before heading to Smyrna she passed through Rome, where she wangled from the Countess Elizabeth a fifteen-minute visit with her children, but no more than that. It was the last time Evelina would see her mother for many years.

Once in Smyrna, Marionca ignored James's conditions and decided to continue on to Constantinople in order to confront Julius. There she finally learned that Julius had already remarried a young widow who was rich enough to sport jewels and own houses.

On hearing that his half-mad first wife was in the neighborhood, Julius—convinced that his entire family, and not only his father, had encouraged Marionca to come out of anger with him—decided upon a new plan: to offer Marionca a small annuity. For the rest of her life she could receive 150 French francs monthly from Julius, but only on condition that she live neither in Turkey nor Italy. Behind this offer was Julius's fear that Marionca's real purpose in coming to Constantinople, where her sister lived, incidentally, was to kidnap little James. It was then that Julius decided to send the four-year-old boy, James, to live in Rome with his mother and sister and his two older siblings, Evelina and Frederick.

In suspecting Marionca of planning a kidnap, Julius was on target, for Marionca then set out to return to Rome as speedily as possible, so as to make, as she later admitted, "one last attempt to snatch them [the children] from the grasp of that wicked woman who had so usurped my rights." From Constantinople, Marionca traveled by ship to Messina—this time, fairly rapidly on the new steamship called "the packet." From Messina, she made her way to Rome.

Evelina and Frederick had remained outside this fray and settled into their new life. As Cornelia wrote, after only thirteen months in Rome, Evelina had won a prize at school. "Evelina was first in her class for geography. What do you think [of] this big little woman? For in her class there are girls of 8 years of age and she is not yet seven."

But then Marionca reappeared in Rome, where she had rented a house for a month. On learning this, an appalled Cornelia wrote Julius on Oct. 22, 1838:

> We warned the masters and mistresses of the children in case she came, not to let her see the children, but she did not try to see them, because she must have known quite well that we absolutely did not want her to. The children did not know at all that Marionca was in Rome, nor will they know. We took great precautions for Eveline, and day and night we trembled for these dearest children whom we love more than if they were our own.
>
> We ... took steps through the authorities to make her leave as soon as possible.

Indeed, Elizabeth made good use of her papal contacts. On learning that her crazed desperado daughter-in-law had turned up in Rome, Elizabeth managed to have Marionca seized by police and held under arrest until papal gendarmes conducted her to the frontier. As long as the pope was king, Marionca could never return to Rome; she was forever formally a persona non grata.

At that point, Marionca, still short of money and with no resources of her own, set out for Paris, where her husband's banker held Julius's promised letters of credit. Arriving there, however, she was stunned to learn from his banker that she must sign an additional agreement, which stipulated that she must either accept the divorce brought by Julius or receive no funds, ever. Only if she accepted (so she related) would she receive from Julius the promised lifetime pension. She chose the money.

For the moment, there was still no trace of that promised money, and so, until it arrived, Marionca decided her sole recourse was to contact the Turkish ambassador to beg a free passage so that she might return home to Constantinople. Taking pity on the woman victimized by the Catholics, the Turkish ambassador took Marionca under his wing. Through his courtesy, and embassy parties, she made the acquaintance of a handsome military attaché of embassy named Mehmet Kibrizli. His polite advances to her were "soon followed by an offer of marriage."

Kibrizli swept Marionca off her feet, and in no time, she had accepted the offer, she related, in hopes of being able "to forget the miseries of a marriage that was more than unhappy." The couple—"betrothed," but not yet married—then left Paris together for Constantinople. Only a year after being hounded out of Rome, Marionca had converted to Islam, and was living again in a palace, Haider-Effendi, together with some 20 other women, all relatives of her betrothed.

This was a proper harem, she related in her memoir, in which the women all lived together in amusing harmony. She resided together with "fifteen or twenty ladies—mothers, step-mothers, aunts, sisters, cousins, step-sisters, and other relatives of the master of the house." Her new abode was spacious and luxuriously furnished, and in it the women "passed the time very pleasantly together, in conversation, dancing, music, listening to and telling stories; in fact, seeking to entertain ourselves in every way we could imagine."[8]

On an unusually dull evening during Ramadan, a Circassian woman, also in the harem, suggested that she and Marionca dress up as boys and go out for an evening. Said her new friend: "We will go together to St. Sophia, to see the festival which is held to-night."

Putting on male apparel, and carrying small lanterns, we went to the mosque. On entering it we were completely dazzled. The columns were decked from top to bottom, with lustres of coloured glass; the Sultan's band was performing; and the crowd was so dense that it was almost impossible to get in.

In the crowd, however, they were noticed, and two real youths tried to coax them into a café. At this, the phony "boys" fled.

This, then, was Marionca's new life.

Four years later, when the newly wed Marionca seemed safely distant and under the care of Pasha Kibrizli, Julius decided that it was high time for his children in Rome to return home to Constantinople to be together with the brood from his second marriage. It was 1842.

His mother's reply was a flat no: she would keep the three children. The Ottoman world was no place to raise Catholic children.

This deepened the rift between Julius and his mother, but fostered some improvement in his relations with his father, who was finally, if belatedly, informed of the existence of his son's second family. On March 10, 1840, James wrote from Florence that he was surprised that Julius would now be married to a Greek woman after his previous "experience with natives," by which he meant the half-French, half-Armenian Marionca.

More reproaches from Julius came the following September: "You never mentioned that your new wife was a widow with three children, nor that you are sending James [the youngest child by Marionca] to a R. C. [Roman Catholic] school. Afraid you are influenced by sordid motives."

In the same letter, the elder James confirmed what Marionca had understood about Elizabeth's money problems. They were now worse, however, for somehow one of her two pensions had abruptly disappeared:

> You know that your mother's financial situation is bad—she having lost a portion of her pension and living in likelihood of retiring to a convent for life, and yet [you] have not sent her any money for the children. Hence she must have recourse to strangers to provide for them as paupers, and yet you say your finances are in a flourishing condition, and you offer to assist me if required.

At that point, however, Julius, who seems to have been an inveterate miser, may have been refusing to send his mother maintenance money for the children as a form of blackmail, with the aim of forcing Elizabeth to send the three to Constantinople. But Elizabeth continued to refuse; instead, evidently to reduce expenses, she left the flat in Palazzo Odescalchi to move into more modest quarters on Monte Cavallo, giving the official reason that they had sublet the flat in the palazzo from a "good Lord Clifton," whose sister was coming to Rome and wanted it.

James took vicious delight in this turn of events, but was shocked when his son Julius admitted callously that his marriage to Marionca had never been fully legal. In a letter dated Jan. 17, 1841, James wrote that he was stunned that Julius would confess that he had sent his wife to his mother and "virgin sister" without warning them of how badly Marionca tended to behave. In addition, "You state that [Marionca] was never your wife; this I never could expect, as you wrote to me invoking my blessing on your union. How could you wish this, after having violated a Sacrament by celebrating it in a manner you knew and intended to be illegal?"

Through all this, Cornelia continued to maintain friendly relations with her brother, primarily for the children's sake. As she wrote fondly in late March of 1838, "In February Evelina received a prize for diligence in her class. She is more studious than before, etc., and so are her two little brothers. We were very worried about James, who caught scarlet fever so badly that we feared to lose him during the first days of February. Now he is very well and the illness has improved him in colour, he is gay, fat and has grown. ... Fred is studying Latin."

Enclosed was a letter from Evelina to her "dearest father." It had been written early in January or even before that, but not sent before March 23 of 1839 because Aunt Cornelia had been too busy to arrange posting it. In another touching letter dated February 1839, Evelina wrote her father:

"I am now in the 4th class [of the Sacré Coeur convent school] and this year my teachers are a little more contented with my studies," Evelina wrote. "I hope I shall continue to be attentive to give them pleasure and to Aunt who is so good to me. I see her often, and also Grandma when she is well." The letter concludes: "Accept, Papa, all my most respectful sentiments, I kiss your hand and ask for your blessing."

Shortly afterward, Cornelia wrote once again, saying that Evelina would like her father to send her a pendant and was hoping, in return, to send Julius a sample of her lace work, "but at the moment is busy at household things, such as sewing."

However piloted the letter may have been, these provide the first direct knowledge we have of Evelina's own thoughts and personality while she was still in boarding school with the *Dames Françaises*. We also learn that Grandma Elizabeth, living in ever more reduced circumstances, was in poor health.

Despite their differences, over the course of the next year, relations between father and son continued to be on the mend, even as Elizabeth continued to refuse to send the children to their father in Constantinople. James had previously written Julius that the children "should be removed from Rome where they are ruined by over indulgence by their grandmother and Cornelia. They have already made Frederick a little tiger."[9]

Elizabeth replied to James in mid-1841, saying that, "I do not believe in all conscience that I have any obligation to deprive myself by restitution of the children left to me spontaneously after the departure of [Julius's] wife." This reply, wrote James to their son, showed that his estranged wife is "as silly as might be expected of her" and moreover, Elizabeth was acting on the basis of the "odious doctrine" she had adopted, Roman Catholicism. James, writing Julius, then threatened to disinherit his son unless Julius would personally tackle the Vatican so as to have his children removed from the clutches of the pope.[10]

Instead of waiting for Julius to do just that, James himself made an appeal to the Vatican. The response was predictably negative, for, as a Curia *apparatchik* pointed out, the children's father, Julius van Millingen, had sent all three of his children to Rome, where he placed them in a convent to be educated. Julius, moreover, was a rich man, but had failed to provide for the maintenance of his own children.

In referring the official Church opinion to his son Julius, James, suggesting that the Catholic Church was always evil, wrote that, as was well known, "The Popes trampled on the necks of Emperors."[11]

By 1842, their quarrels were definitively behind James and his son Julius, who joined forces in their wrath directed against Elizabeth. Deciding to bring the matter before the public, they wrote a 41-page pamphlet, which they had published in London. The title of the pamphlet was "Arbitrary Detention by the Inquisition at Rome of three Protestant Children in Defiance of the Will of their Father." In the pamphlet, Julius—in fact, his father James, its real author—accused the Vatican Inquisition of holding his three children prisoner.

Even more peculiar, given that James was a respected antiquarian, was the wild accusation in the pamphlet that, together with agents of the Inquisition, granny Elizabeth had concocted a plot alleging that their mother, Marionca, was an adulteress. This was a blatant lie about Marionca invented by Elizabeth (so said the pamphlet) to justify kidnapping the children, who were detained under the "pretense of the danger of intrusting (sic) them to the care of a guilty mother." It is safe to doubt that Marionca, back in the Kislizi's harem in Constantinople, knew anything of her redemption in this pamphlet.

Julius (that is, James, who had now obtained power of attorney from his son) then directly contacted the Vatican Secretary of State to ask for the children's extradition. When the Vatican ignored this newest appeal, James applied to the British ambassador to Florence, who similarly rebuffed him, arguing that the mother of the children, Marionca, may well have more right to claim them than did Julius.

James's next step was to seek the advice of lawyers in Rome, who responded that the case fell under canon law since the children had "embraced" the Catholic faith. This left little chance that they would be released to an Ottoman world, not to mention to the hands of their father, a divorced man.

At that point, James and his son learned from a Roman banker that the pope himself had "appointed Prince Pietro Odescalchi as tutor to the children, and they are no longer under the care of their grandmother. I have spoken to the Prince, who is a friend of mine, and bears an excellent character."

Stubborn James would not accept this. That April, he appealed to the Earl of Aberdeen to ask Her Majesty's Government to compel Elizabeth to renounce "care" of the children. This too failed. As the Earl explained, the Government cannot be expected to interfere in what is a private matter. "It does not appear to the Earl of Aberdeen that either your son or yourself have taken the measure necessary for accomplishing the object you profess to have in view."[12]

Finally, Julius appealed directly to the Pope. In a letter addressed to the "Holy Father" and dated May 14, 1848, Julius wrote from Constantinople that he was bereaved, "alone and in sack cloth" because of being denied his paternal rights, and insinuated that the pontiff represented "unrighteousness." He reminded the pontiff that the Sultan himself [Julius's capital letter] had written on Julius's behalf asking for the return of the children.

There was no reply.

From Florence, James battled on nevertheless. Ignoring the negative reply he had received from the Earl of Aberdeen, this latest letter was a renewed attempt to have the question brought before Parliament. In his son's name, James insinuated that the Earl had urged Julius to use violence:

> Having resorted to every step, except going in person to Rome and violently contending with my mother and sister for the possession of my children, I must conclude that his lordship [the Earl of Aberdeen] hinted the propriety of doing so. If I thought that there were the slightest probability of this measure being conducive to the attainment of my wishes, I should at once adopt it.
>
> But, judging from the bigotry and fanaticism of my mother, I feel confident that on my arrival at Rome the children would at once be placed beyond my reach, and that, if I made much noise, a Roman stiletto would free my adversaries from my importunities. Catholics have no scruples when the arm of religion directs their blows.

Phew! A Roman stiletto? Small wonder that the editors of the English Catholic weekly *The Tablet*, in an article of Oct. 22, 1842, ridiculed the author of the pamphlet, as well as all the characters mentioned in it, as "a confederation of fools and knaves." The author—clearly of a most "peculiar Protestant morality"—combined "falsehood, slander and nonsense into ... the blustering lie of an unscrupulous man in a violent passion."

In the end, nothing came of the appeals to attorneys and politicians. The children remained in Rome. However poverty-stricken their grandmother, she had not yet faded away into a convent and did not release the children to their (presumably) Godless Protestant father.

From those years, a single letter survives, written by Evelina to her father in an elegant hand, and obviously copied carefully from a draft. The letter, dated 10 October 1845, was written in Italian (she apologizes for not writing in French) when she was fourteen years old. In it she addresses Julius in the polite, third person singular, "Lei," rather than the familiar "tu." She thanks her father for having sent her a little portrait of himself, "though I don't find that it resembles you"—not that she had seen him for a decade. The previous day she and her aunt had visited her brothers in their seminary, she wrote.

Then Evelina changes the subject: the news which a certain Madame Dumont—obviously an intermediary between the children and their father—had conveyed to her about her father was a genuine "consolation," but then this Madame Dumont had left Rome, and, "I did not write you about it because, after my having sent her a cap, she did not even reply, and I thought that she did not want to write me anymore, and I no longer had the courage to [write her]." Even so, I did not forget her, Evelina continues, for, "I love her tenderly, and am praying for her." Grandmother Elizabeth and Aunt Cornelia, moreover, had now given Evelina books that had belonged to her father—"orations and books for study plus the *petit pulpitre* [little desktop] upon which you wrote when you were a boy."

"Your most obedient and affectionate daughter Evelina," she concluded in Italian, adding in French, "I kiss your hands."

Cornelia was also conscientiously keeping in touch, writing in early 1846 that the children were well, "advancing in studies, and they kiss your hand." But then she added sorrowfully, "Mama is not answering you because the style of your letter has too deeply hurt the heart of a mother who loves you so much."

Julius was still being a tightwad, as a letter Augustus wrote his brother that same year, 1846, evinces. In it, Augustus sagely suggests that, "In order that your children may preserve their affection for you, you must occasionally send them some presents and even a little pocket money."

That same year, their father, James, died in Florence. Julius and Augustus, the two brothers, had not seen each other for 25 years. But now they wrote cordially to each other to discuss their inheritance, and also Julius's ever more desperate attempts to have his three children returned to his care. In his own letter to Julius dated January 23, 1846, Augustus writes:

My mother, under the influence of a fanatical zeal, has firmly persuaded herself that it is an imperative duty which has devolved to her from heaven. … You ought to consider your children as prisoners; they have not now power to break their chains, but will have it 'ere long. They live without their knowledge on charity, and this galls me to the quick.

Keep this in confidence, Augustus adds, "Keep it secret."

Rumbles of revolution were sweeping the North of Italy, far from the Papal States which cut a swath across Central Italy. Control of the Northeast was under pro-Catholic Austria while the South and Sicily were independent as the Kingdom of the Two Sicilies. In addition, there were three duchies in North-Central Italy.

Rome began to see turmoil after 1840. When a new pope was elected in June 1846 as Pius IX, it was hoped that this unrest would be quelled, but instead the situation grew worse. By April of 1848, papal troops were obliged to try to defend the city gates.

During that revolutionary year of 1848, Elizabeth van Millingen died on August 11. It was, Cornelia wrote Julius, a "calm and peaceful death," and their mother's last words were, "I bless Julius." Evelina and her brothers were "shattered" by the death of their grandmother, Cornelia added.

Because the children were boarders living in convent schools, they were to some extent shielded from their grandmother's death. But money was ever more lacking, and worse was to come. The center of historical Rome is small, and there can be no doubt the children, and the nuns tending them, were also shattered by the events taking place all around them, including food riots. Not even cloistered nuns could ignore the fighting that had begun in the streets of Rome.

As revolution closed in upon Rome, a minister for the papal court was murdered by an Italian patriot on November 15, 1848. At that point, Austrian troops forced their way through Tuscany and then, aggressively, headed toward Rome, where the pope refused to counterattack with his own troops, on grounds Austria was an ally as a fellow Catholic nation. As the war widened, mobs of Roman university students and well-heeled bourgeois called for the pope to abdicate in mid-November of 1848, but the pope refused, stating, "I do not have the right."

Only a few days later, an armed mob dragged a cannon into the piazza in front of the Quirinal Palace and tried to fire it. In the fracas, a monsignor was killed, and on November 24, the pope fled from Rome to take refuge in a fortress at Gaeta under the protection of the King of Naples and the Two Sicilies.

A year had passed since the death of grandmother Elizabeth. On February 26, 1849, an alarmed Julius set out at last from Constantinople in an effort to rescue the children personally. Reaching Rome, he was present that April, when the uprising turned even more violent. Some 6,000 French soldiers, who had left their ships of war at the Roman port of Civitavecchia, forced their way into Rome and attacked the patriots and Vatican soldiers trying to defend the city. The fighting went from the Janiculum Hill down to the Cavalleggeri Gate, adjacent to St. Peter's Basilica.

Meanwhile, according to a family history, Julius's younger brother, Augustus, who was still living in Albano, had become friends with some of the revolutionaries now running Rome in the absence of the pope. Augustus is said to have smoothed the way toward the release of the children into the hands of their father, and to providing them exit permits from the papal state.

Armed with documents, Julius and Augustus together presented themselves at the school the boys attended, the Collegio Romano, a Jesuit seminary just a few steps across Via del Corso from Palazzo Odescalchi.[13] Their father was introduced to the two adolescent boys, whom he had not seen for many years. Both were dressed like clerics.

The problems did not end immediately: "The Rector could not resist [oppose] the official documents for transfer of the boys. But, by coincidence as they were leaving, Evelina and their aunt appeared, barring their exit. An agonizing scene ensued. "In despair Aunt Cornelia called on Julius to leave the boys, but their father and uncle bundled them into the carriage," reads a family history. Evelina was by then a handsome eighteen years of age, Frederick seventeen, James fifteen.

Aunt Cornelia, deep in grief from her mother's death and now at the prospect of losing the children she loved, mustered support from the upper crust Roman nobility including—so Frederick later recalled—members of the Colonna, Torlonia, and Bentivoglio families. Julius and his younger brother had taken rooms at the Hotel Condotti, where they were visited by these Roman aristocrats, who "saw it as their duty to come and console our aunt"—and to try to talk Julius out of removing the children from Rome.

Money to maintain Julius's lonely sister, as well as her genuine love for the children after thirteen years of caring for them, was obviously also an issue. In the end, following visits from Torlonia and Colonna family members, a compromise was found. Aunt Cornelia should join Julius's new and enlarged household in Constantinople, where she would continue as governess to children already too old for a governess. In a major concession to his sister Cornelia and her aristocratic Catholic friends, Julius also promised to respect the children's Catholic religion.

4

Constantinople

On April 2, 1849, as Augustus stayed on in Rome, the five set sail from the port of Gaeta, south of Rome, to Malta and onward to Constantinople and their new life in the heart of the Ottoman Empire.

Twelve years had elapsed since five-year-old Evelina had boarded the sailing vessel that bore her from Constantinople to Rome. The voyage had taken four months; by the time she returned to her father's home in 1849 at age eighteen, the sailing vessels on that long route were being replaced by iron steamships, like the *Hellespont*. Owned by the General Screw Steam Shipping Co. Ltd., it made its maiden voyage from Liverpool to Gibraltar and Malta, ending in Constantinople in just four weeks, one quarter of the time it had taken Evelina and her brother to reach Central Italy thirteen years previously.

To England, the *Hellespont* bore such delicacies as dates, olive oil, and "2 boxes opium" (to quote the ship's manifest). The speedier new steamships also fostered middle-class tourism between Constantinople and Western Europe, and this introduced new cultural concepts. To a certain extent, it was a two-way traffic: the leaders of the Ottoman Empire sought European-style industrial modernization while a certain echelon of the British and French middle class, after a century of living amidst factories, looked Eastward for what they considered an exotic lifestyle.

To these Westerners, Constantinople appeared the very essence of this, and by mid-century, travel to the city had become a vogue among Western middle-class tourists, female as well as male. Publication of their travel diaries generated more tourism, and more diaries. The first influential female diarist was Lady Mary Wortley Montagu (1689-1762), whose British husband, a Whig Member of Parliament, was sent to Turkey as ambassador. One year after her death, an unauthorized, limited edition of her journal entries and compiled letters (written mostly to her daughter) were published as *Letters of the Right Honourable Lady M-y W-y M-e*.

In 1837, the book was republished as *Letters and Works* and reached a broader readership. Male readers delighted in Lady Montagu's *Letters* for their unwittingly titillating descriptions of Turkish women in the bath house and the harem; as Montagu correctly reminded readers, no male visitor had been an intimate of the world of women in Constantinople—but she had. At the same time, the success of the book, along with its style and subject matter, encouraged other English women not only to travel, but also to write and publish their diaries.

Although the van Millingens did not leave diaries, these mid-nineteenth century travelers, plus the lithographers and early photographers, evoke the life of Constantinople and of Evelina herself. The women's diaries, moreover, illuminate the world of Evelina's mother, Marionca, who would ultimately enter a harem and leave lengthy descriptions of it.

Montagu herself was fairly down to earth. On the one hand, she wrote that the harem housed "the only women in the world that lead a life of uninterrupted pleasure exempt from cares; the whole time being spent in visiting, bathing, or in the agreeable amusement of spending money, and inventing new fashions." On the other hand, Montagu specified, "A husband would be thought mad that exacted any degree of economy from his wife, whose expenses are in no way limited but by her own fancy. It is his business to get money, and hers to spend it." (Marionca intuitively had understood this; Julius had not.)

After Montagu, Julia Pardoe (1806-1862) from Yorkshire was an influential woman traveler and diarist. Pardoe's book *The Beauties of the Bosphorus* appeared, with illustrations, in 1838, just one year after Montagu's *Letters*. In it she recounts her voyage the previous year to Turkey with her father, Major Thomas Pardoe. Like Montagu, Pardoe had gained access to the harem world, which helped to make her book remarkably successful as a popularizer of the exotic Orient.

Another influential writer was Albert Richard Smith (1816-1860), a doctor clever enough with a pen to be an occasional contributor to *Punch*. Smith traveled to Constantinople with his wife at roughly the same time as did the van Millingen children, 1849, and along the same Mediterranean route. His book describing his travels, *A Month at Constantinople*, became so successful that he subsequently gave up the practice of medicine to become a full-time travel writer and lecturer.

Captain Charles White was another visitor to Turkey. His book, *Three Years in Constantinople; or, Domestic Manners of the Turks*, appeared in England in 1844. In its Volume Three, White, discussing "Conjugal Rights determined by Kooran," explains engagingly that a sultan's female establishment was composed of 350 or so women, from the Valide Sultana at the top of the heap down to the ladies-in-waiting who purveyed sweets to the harem women and their female visitors. Like the other male writers, White had never seen or been inside a harem, but his detailed harem depictions were gobbled up by Western readers; it scarcely mattered that they were largely fantasy, for no one could disprove them.

Supplementing the travel diaries were engravings like those of French lithographer Gaspare Fossati (1809-1883), whose visual record from the 1850s of Hagia Sofia (Aya Sofia in Turkish) and the old covered market is considered a landmark, and is still popular today. In the 1840s, artist James Robertson, already known for his fine engravings of Constantinople, took up photography and opened his own photo studio there in 1854.[2] Both his engravings and photographs illustrated the great sights of Constantinople: the Hagia Sofia, the Mosque of Sultan Ahmet, and the gate and fountain of the old palace. All this further popularized Turkey; among his clients was Prince Albert.

After the ship bearing the van Millingens—Evelina, her two younger brothers, her aunt Cornelia, and her father—had passed Smyrna (Izmir), it followed the coastline in a northeasterly direction through the elongated Dardanelles Strait into the Sea of Marmara. From there they caught their first distant glimpse of Constantinople, with its "white buildings and lofty minarets glittering in the sun," to borrow Dr. Smith's description from the same vantage point.

The city that had been ancient Byzantium was now home to over 800,000, and its port swarmed with life. The waterfront was a maelstrom of "wherries" (small canal boats with sails), which delivered goods, and of barges heaped with melons, fur pelts, bales of hay, and grain. The steamer in which Dr. Smith had sailed was given a special welcome by two "imposing" Turkish customs officers, who had approached alongside in a gilded barge and announced they were there for an inspection. Paid a bribe of just three piastres ("a little more than sixpence"), the inspectors dropped the inspection, only to speed away to another European steamer which might be fleeced.

But never mind. As his ship entered port at Constantinople, Dr. Smith waxed ecstatic at sight of:

> Quaint houses, and intermingled foliage, and graceful cypress groves that climbed to the very summits of the hills, and stretched far away in the distance—the thousand ships that the noble harbour brought alongside the very streets—the fairy palaces commencing to border the Bosphorus—the light gilded wherries that darted by in all directions amidst the tame sea-birds who rode upon the clear rippling water—the gaily-coloured crowds up the bridge—the vivid sunlight—the exhilarating atmosphere.

Bribes and lofty minarets, sea gulls and fairy palaces, domes and opium: this was the schizophrenic Constantinople which awaited Evelina. By "the bridge," Smith meant the Galata Bridge, built only four years before his visit to cross the Golden Horn. The bridge linked the two shores of a 4½-mile-long curving estuary that sliced into the land mass. The two sides were home to two distinct worlds which regarded each other with diffidence. On the one side was the heart of the old city—the larger, low-lying Stamboul, as it was called at the time, home primarily to Muslim Turks. Inhabited by some two-thirds of the population, Stamboul also housed most of the great ancient mosques, the covered bazaars, the officious government buildings, and, not least, the sultans' palaces with their harems, the seraglio. Smith, for one, remarked upon the number of street peddlers while ogling the veiled women.

Like the houses of other foreign residents, the home in which Evelina was to live was on the opposite side of the Golden Horn from Stamboul, in hilly Pera, which the Turks knew as Beyoğlu. In this polyglot, Westernized quarter, the inhabitants were collectively known as "Levantines." Pera began at the port with the low-lying hodgepodge neighborhood called Galata, a place of "dirty shops for ships' stores, merchants' counting-houses, and tipsy sailors," Smith recorded. Here Marionca had grown up.

From Galata, broad stairstep streets scrambled uphill to Pera proper, the prosperous garden district set high on bluffs overlooking the sea. Its mansions had been built by the English, near elegant hotels frequented by European businessmen and tourists; the sultan himself had decreed that no hotels should be built on the Muslim Stamboul side.

For the young ones, the adjustment did not appear easy at the outset. Frederick wrote that, "We were shocked by the torturous alleys at Galata, the sinister-looking men, the dogs, the animals of all kinds, the weird costumes of a thousand colors and bizarre shapes. My sister Evelina had to make a superhuman effort to squelch the sense of disgust she felt at sight of Pera, her new home, her improvised father."[3]

Among the businessmen ensconced in Pera were Greek bankers, important because they handled money on behalf of the Ottoman rulers, who could not. Pera's Grand Rue was a lively boulevard of "noisy shops" run by French and Italian merchants, by Persians selling sheepskins, carpets, and shawls, and by the clever Germans who had cornered the market on sales of crockery and glass goblets with covers.

There were enough foreign families to require a dozen or so schools where teaching was in various languages. Many were church-related for both Roman Catholics and Protestants; one school was specifically for American Protestants. Constantinople was also home to 55,000 Jews, of whom 5,000 lived between Galata and Pera. Hugging the bridge at Galata was a synagogue, one of several serving the community.[4]

The elegance of the hillside, despite the garden mansions of the ambassadors, was relative, however. Roads were paved with "all sorts of ragged stones, jammed down together without any regard to a level surface," Smith recorded. Dead rats, melon rinds, stray dogs, rags, brickbats, and rubbish littered the streets in front of unkempt wooden houses, and "Even the better class of houses had an uncared-for, mouldy, plague-imbued, decaying look about them."[5]

Pera was also home to large military contingents—one with 1,000 horses—and military hospitals. Another barracks, the Selimya, straddled the heights atop Pera overlooking the sea, and had space for 4,000 horses and 12,000 men. The building stood three stories tall, and had four tall corner towers and 2,000 windows.

Maltepe, on the Sea of Marmara, sheltered yet another gigantic barracks and hospital. Showing that Julius's position as a foreign doctor was not unusual, Captain White explains that the Turkish medical practitioners were "ignorant" and so had to be flanked by a contingent of German and a dozen or so Jewish doctors, all of whom had been trained abroad.[6] The illnesses they treated were primarily gastro-intestinal, White wrote in 1844; this would presumably have been as true inside the palaces where Julius was in attendance as in the barracks.

One element which visitors invariably noticed with pleasure, White writes, was the beauty of the children and their sensible clothing: "The tight shackles, so often fatal to the health of European girls, are unknown. This freedom, combined with their flowing robes, gives to them an air of ease, roundness, and self-possession that cannot be attained by aid of stays, backboards and dancing-masters."[7]

Given their different religions, customs, and history, the two cities, Stamboul and Pera, did not always understand one another. It was in Evelina's time in Constantinople when a Miss Emmeline Lott, working as governess for little Prince Ibrahim, found it awkward when she and her ward, strolling along the Bosphorus, noticed a basket floating by. In it was the severed head of a woman, presumably an unfaithful wife. "It was difficult [for Miss Lott] to explain to the boy what the poor ladies had done to have their heads cut off," wrote Robert Liddell in *Byzantium and Istanbul*.[8] That book is contemporary, but Lott herself wrote, in *The English Governess in Egypt; Harem Life in Egypt and Constantinople*, published in 1867, that the little prince,

> ... did not dislike the Franks, but he abhorred those unclean beasts! those misbelieving dogs! —the Jews; and on one day, when he pointed his little hand to a headless corpse that we saw floating by a caique which lay at anchor in the stream, he inquired of me, if that were not the body of a *kopek*, "dog of an Israelite?" I replied that I did not know. *Basham itchiam*, "By my head!" *jehenum*, "Hell will be the portion of that accursed band, as there is but one Allah," added the little Pacha, clapping his tiny hands.

Describing the life of the women in the harem, Lott wrote:

> The ladies of the Sultan's Harem were much more civilized than those of the Viceroy's ; for they amused themselves of an evening singing songs to their own accompaniments on castanets; while others sat quietly in a group, not like the dames of olden

times, plying at their distaffs and spindles, but industriously employed in useful needlework, repairing their own garments; others again played at cards and dominoes;—all smoking, and sipping coffee out of zarfs [cup holders] of gold, encrusted with diamonds.[9]

In England, at about this same time, women like Miss Lott, and men as well, were reading novels which portrayed a quite different sort of male-female relationship. Charlotte Brontë's *Jane Eyre*, first published in 1847, tells the story of the orphaned child Jane who grows up to become a governess, like Miss Lott. But Jane is also able to become a cultivated woman who refuses Mr. Rochester's offer to make her his second wife, because his mad first wife is still alive. She also declines to be his mistress. Her head was not cut off, nor that of his first wife.

On the other hand, some of the English did not like the Jane Eyre style of female independence. For traveler Gordon Trenery, Turkish women were "instinctively delicate, and fraught with female holiness: ... you cannot be with her long, without feeling soothed, exalted and having your heart filled with greater love for your kind." At the same time, he kept his fantasies sufficiently in check to describe a particularly gory incident he witnessed during his visit to Constantinople in 1854.

> A stifled shriek rose upon the quiet air. It had not died away when he heard a dull, heavy splash. A woman confined in a sack, that was fastened round her neck, was flung from the caique into the Bosphorus ... There the poor young creature still floated; her eyes were closed, her long hair was spread out upon the dark waves. She did not sink immediately, and the officers in the caique were pushing her under by their oars. She had been the favourite wife of an elderly merchant, and had been given her choice of poison, the [garrot] or drowning.[10]

On one occasion in Constantinople's deep past, 300 women had been dispatched, all at the same time. But if only one or two women were drowned, the event attracted little notice, N. M. Penzer wrote in his history of the harem, published in 1936, when the institution had been gone for only a quarter century, and first-hand memories of it were still fresh. Carried out "with silence and dispatch," the women would be taken to a *Bostanji-bashi*.

> Under [his] direction the hapless females are placed in sacks weighted with stones. The *bostanji*, to whom the duty of drowning them is committed, board a small rowing-boat to which is attached by rope a smaller one in which the women are placed. They then row towards the open water opposite Seraglio Point, and by several dexterous jerks of the rope cause

the boat to capsize. A eunuch accompanies the *bostanji* and reports to the Kislar Agha the fulfillment of his orders.[11]

The arrival of the van Millingen children in Pera caused a happy stir among Dr. van Millingen's friends and acquaintances in the Greek, English, and Protestant communities, where there was noisy rejoicing over the (presumed) humiliation of the Catholic Pope who had been forced to flee from Rome.

Julius's family had expanded considerably since Evelina had left so many years before. Marionca had signed away her right to live in Turkey or Italy, and Julius had married his longtime mistress, the 25-year-old butcher's widow. Saphiriza (also known as Zafira) Ralli had brought to the marriage two children of her own before adding more with Julius. The two had met when Julius was called to her bedside when she was ill.

Julius's divorce had come fairly easily because the Greek Orthodox Church in Pera was unauthorized to marry subjects who were not Greek. Neither Marionca nor Julius being Greek, their marriage was thus considered invalid under British law (although whether British law would apply to Turkey was questionable, as was whether Julius was cynical enough to have known this before marrying the teenaged Marionca).[12]

Carrying this argument onward, it was argued that Marionca's marriage to Julius had never been valid, and hence the children from that marriage, beginning with Evelina, were illegitimate under British law. Thus, in 1840, he could marry Saphiriza because their wedding figured technically in England as Julius's first—even though he did not obtain a Turkish divorce from Marionca until June 1848, seven years after he married Saphiriza.

Their wedding took place in the British Embassy, where it was officiated by John Brabazon Ponsonby, the English ambassador who had replaced Canning in 1833.

Shortly after marrying Saphiriza, Julius had unexpectedly received a letter from none other than Miss Robertson, the woman who had broken his heart in Edinburgh. She was writing, she said, after having read his *Memoirs of the Affairs of Greece*, and wished to tell him how much she regretted having given in to her brother, and had ever after held Julius in her heart. Despite his "unrelenting silence," she suggested that they reconnect.

I heard of your being in Paris, of your being in London, and, oh, you may imagine whether I expected you to visit Scotland. It was not until after reading your book, and writing Mr. Rodwell to ask where the author was, that my hopes of seeing you vanished, and not having calculated on the possibility of disappointment, I cannot express to you its effects ... I must restrain my desire of communing more at length with you as doubtless you have received my many former letters.

She concluded by letting him know the dates when she planned to be in Edinburgh, where she hoped to see him. The letter ended with the tender words, "Farewell, my ever dear Julius."

Had he received all those former letters? This remains uncertain. Painfully Julius responded that it was not to be: her letter, inspired by her reading his *Memoirs*, had arrived too late, and he had just been married.

Then Saphiriza herself died of tuberculosis ("consumption") on July 23, 1843. She was only 29 years old, but had already borne Julius three children. The first was Alexander, born in 1840, who would become a famous historian of Islamic architecture. The following year twins were born; one, John, died in infancy, while the other, Charles, survived and grew up to become a doctor working in Persia.

This means that even as Julius was pleading with his mother in Rome to have his three children by Marionca returned to him, he was already obliged to care for the four already in Istanbul: the late Saphiriza's two from her first marriage, plus two-year-old Alexander and one-year-old Charles. Saphiriza's death left Julius "in a state of embarrassment," as one of his sons later recalled; he was not only free to remarry, but in desperate need of a wife to manage his overblown household.

It happened that just three months before Saphiriza died, Julius had received yet another letter from his old lost love in Scotland, Miss Robertson. Her letter of March 3, 1843, reminded him that he had last written her no less than five years previously, in August of 1828. "Every day brings us news of tidings of the wars and the threatened dangers of Constantinople," she wrote. "Oh Julius how you do, how you are situated, and if you are likely to absent yourself all your life from Britain; and oh do add that you think of me sometimes with affection."

He did think of her, and of marriage to her, as a brief flutter of letters soon made clear. In a tender letter dated Oct. 14, 1845, Julius wrote that his never forgotten dream of happiness of the past 25 years might now be realized, if she might accept "the proposals I once ventured to make, but which my evil destiny led you to reject."

> It is now three years since I became a widower ... [Do] become mine own—
> shed rays of happiness over the remaining portion of the gloomy existence I
> have led because separated from you. I will be presumptuous enough to say
> you cannot, you will not refuse me.

If she would have him, Julius even considered transferring back to England. She would not. Too much time had passed: she missed him, but at 59 she was older than he, and had not previously realized that seven children would accompany him wherever he went. Only three years had passed since she had written Julius a come-hither letter, but now, on Feb. 4, 1846, an older and wiser

Miss Robertson wrote starchily that, "I do not see the slightest possibility of our ever being more than we at present are to each other. ... I am in no manner of way qualified to take the charge of such a family as yours."

"And now, my dear Sir," she wrote, "I must say Adieu and beg you will allow this correspondence to drop. It is best for both of us"—that correspondence which she had herself revived.

On August 2, 1847, Julius was married for the third time, presuming that the marriage to Marionca is counted. This wedding was held at the British Embassy in Constantinople, and his new bride was Adelaide La Fontaine, nineteen years his junior. He had first seen Adelaide as a baby at the home of her banker father in Smyrna, where her Huguenot family of Calvinists had fled from persecution in Catholic France. A widow with two little daughters, she was, like the late Saphiriza, fairly well-to-do. She was notably sensible, energetic, and kind, as well as extremely devout. "She came as an angel of mercy into my father's household," wrote their son Edwin.[13] According to a family account, she provided Julius with a much-needed religious "re-education."

Julius moved his ever-expanding family into a wooden house situated near the elegant new British Embassy in the Ainali Cheshme quarter of Pera. That embassy was spectacular: sheltering amidst a grove of cypress trees, it was designed in emulation of the Tuscan Gothic style of Palazzo Pitti in Florence by W. J. Smith, architect of the Reform Club in London.

This was the home to which the three van Millingen children and their aunt were taken upon their arrival in Constantinople. Frederick has left a description of his, Evelina's, and James's first glance at their new home, an "immense wooden cage" with many windows:

> Despite our age we have enough good taste to be seized with horror when we left the ship at Galata and set out through a confused mass of men, dogs and other animals of all kinds. The torturous and narrow noisy streets, the men with sinister figure and the air of business, the strange costumes of a thousand colors and the most bizarre forms produced on us an appalling effect. To reach the doctor's house they [Julius's patients, presumably] had to climb straight up the streets. In front of the doorway was another obstacle, a deep pit filled with all sorts of rubbish.[14]

Much later that wooden house was one of the 5,000 buildings, including the British Embassy, that would be burned to the ground. One thousand people, including many plunderers, died from the fire, which took with it almost all of Julius's personal belongings and books, including the manuscript of the life of Byron he was writing. From there the family moved to Topchillar, into a house, itself later to be burned down in 1869.

At that point Julius bought a giant house on the Bosphorus. The price was extraordinarily low; the house was considered haunted because its original Armenian owner had murdered his wife, chopped her into pieces, and flung her into the Bosphorus inside a sack weighted with stones.

Frederick conceded that his new stepmother, Adelaide, possessed a certain air of distinction and was not without charm. But she was "thin as a rake," and the two daughters from her previous marriage were ugly as sin and "common looking."

As for Evelina, she was deeply unhappy, Frederick wrote with evident gusto:

Our sister Evelina had to make a superhuman effort to stifle the sense of disgust which Pera inspired in her—this new home, this improvised mother. She was just seventeen years old [more likely, eighteen]; at that age precocious girls from the South have a perfect awareness of men and things. In Italy Evelina had already begun to frequent the world, she already had her own head, her tastes and habits were already formed. Also, as was reasonable, she resented even more than we did the effect of this brusk transfer from Rome to Constantinople.[15]

Part of the shock of that brusk transfer would have been the chaos of a household which had come to include a total of eleven children. Besides the three adults, Julius, Adele, and Aunt Cornelia, there was Evelina, Frederick, and the younger James, plus Adele's two daughters from her previous marriage and the two youngsters she bore with Julius: Julius Robertson (known as "J. R."), born in 1848, and Edwin, a future oculist, born in 1850. Perhaps fortunately, at least two of Saphiriza's four children were later sent to live elsewhere, with relatives of their late mother.

In what would condition Frederick's life, at least, he and his younger brother James were put into the military training college of Valata Serai. Evelina continued to be presented to the international high society of Pera at its embassy parties and grand balls.

But in the meantime, however roomy the wooden house with windows in Pera, it must have been confusing for an eighteen-year-old girl who had been raised mostly by nuns in a Roman convent. That confusion may have been horrible or delightful, and probably a bit of both.

For Evelina, however, that house came to matter only relatively, for in Pera, Evelina showed a perhaps surprising adaptability. This former convent girl settled into the cosmopolitan social life of embassy receptions and amusements, and, most importantly for her, made a new friend, the older wife of an Austrian diplomat. More than the convent boarding school in Rome, more than her grandmother and her aunt, that friendship would open for her new vistas of style, of substance, and even of emotion. It would change her entire life.

In his career, Julius was enjoying good fortune, for he had become well introduced into both worlds in Constantinople: the Ottoman world and the Western circles of Pera. Standing six feet tall, with piercing blue eyes, dark hair, and a ruddy moustache, Julius had by then achieved considerable professional distinction. He was a founder of the Medical Society of Constantinople and had been honored by the king of Holland for his work in trying to stamp out the plague and cholera. As a result, he and his family frequented the foreign diplomatic circles, where Julius was made welcome in the English community, including by Ponsonby, and in the Dutch colony as well.

Following in his father's footsteps, Julius cultivated a passion for archaeology, and indeed gave lectures on archeology in Greek, the language he had learned during his daredevil days with the Greek revolutionaries. He had personally discovered ancient ruins in Phrygia and excavated a temple to Jupiter on the Bosphorus. He was president of a literary society, and had launched into his ambitious project of writing a biography of Lord Byron (it was this manuscript which was burned with the wooden house near the British Embassy).

More prosaically, at home in Pera during the morning hours, Adelaide helped her doctor husband tend to the less well-to-do local patients, by helping to prepare the medicines and pills he prescribed.

Julius spent his afternoons across the Golden Horn in service in Stamboul. There, when he was summoned to the Topkapi Palace harem, Julius, like any other doctor, was allowed to see only the hand of the woman patient. In Chapter 35 of his *Memoirs*, Julius had already written a few details about his experience with patients in the harem. In 1826, he related, Ibrahim Pasha had postponed liberating him from palace service because, "all Turks [are] averse to change a physician who has ever been entrusted the care of his harem."

In Stamboul one afternoon, Julius was presented with an unusual patient. The young (and future sultan) Abdul Aziz complained to one Diamandi, head of the Imperial Pharmacy adjacent to Topkapi Palace, that his pet rooster was ill. Diamandi reflected a moment, then suggested that Dr. Julius would be just the right medical person to tend to the rooster. Summoned, Julius examined the patient attentively, then cannily advised Abdul Aziz that the best cure would be an enema, to be administered by pharmacist Diamandi. That evening, Julius retired to his home to snicker in private while smoking his usual four-foot-long pipe of jasmine-scented wood.

Jokes must have been far and few in the palace, for this pleasantry has come down through van Millingen family archives. As the rooster jest shows, Julius's profession had granted him entree into the inner circles of Stamboul, and had made him a welcome and tolerated presence in the Muslim world on the opposite side of the Golden Horn, to the point that he could joke with a future sultan. Paving the way, suggests a van Millingen family researcher, was the publication of his book, *Memoirs of the Affairs of Greece*, which contained some criticism of the Greeks.

Julius's many years in Constantinople had begun under the reformist Sultan Mahmud II, whose long reign, which began in 1808, ended only with his death in 1839. Throughout those 31 years, one of Mahmud's multitude of sisters, the Ottoman princess Esma (1778-1848), stood out among the others for the remarkable and fairly progressive influence she held over her brother, seven years younger. She had been married at age fourteen, and never remarried after her husband died in 1803, when she was 25. Just five years later, her brother became sultan. Esma had a strong and independent personality. Remarkably Westernized by Ottoman standards, she delighted in things British and had one of her palaces outfitted with English furniture.

As she was approaching 60, Esma suffered from acute rheumatism or, more probably, arthritis. Summoned to tend to her ailments, Julius proposed that hot thermal baths would relieve the pain. The extensive thermal baths built by the ancient Romans in Constantinople had fallen into disuse, so Esma simply ordered them reopened under a temporary roof. She also ordered construction of an access road which would allow her personal carriage to reach the baths.

She also suffered from chronic indigestion, which was called at that time "dyspepsia" (perhaps acid reflux). For this, Julius recommended she discontinue eating the coarse local bread in favor of a more delicate variety. She agreed, hiring a baker from Vienna to come to Constantinople to bake yeast-risen bread and rolls for her in a specially built oven. To show her gratitude, Esma gave Julius a fine cashmere shawl.

In 1839, after 31 years on the throne, her brother Mahmud died from tuberculosis. His son, Abdul Mejid, took his father's place as sultan.

Grateful to Julius for having healed his mother, Abdul Mejid appointed Julius the official Court Physician in 1840 and presented him with a diamond-studded coffee cup holder called a *zarf*. Esma and Julius remained close enough that when Julius was campaigning to have the children released from Rome in 1849, Esma wrote a personal letter to Queen Victoria on his behalf.

When he succeeded his father to the throne in 1839, Abdul Mejid was barely sixteen years old. He would rule throughout the years when Evelina lived in Constantinople (four years before her engagement plus one year before she was married). Educated in Europe, Abdul Mejid spoke French—he was the first sultan to do so—and enjoyed Western classical music. Importantly for Turkey, Abdul Mejid emulated his father in initiating important reforms. He attempted to establish an early form of Parliament in 1845; he set up a council for public instruction in 1846; he created paper money; he planned to abolish slave markets (at that time they still existed in the United States); and he created

Turkey's first modern universities and academies in 1848. A decade later, he decriminalized homosexuality and abolished the turban in favor of the fez.

Abdul Mejid's mother was a beautiful Georgian named Bezmialem, who became the Valide Sultan, the equivalent of the British Queen Mother, though more powerful, even in politics. As Valide Sultan, Bezmialem oversaw a huge staff. There was her first secretary (as if this was an embassy), who had her own six assistants; a treasurer with more assistants; a first seal-bearer; a wardrobe mistress, and so on, down to a Mistress of Sherbets and First Coffee Maker, for a total of some 100 women of all ages. Among these were Julius's patients.

The good times would last throughout and beyond the sultanate of Abdul Mejid, who died in 1861 when he was only 39. The official version is that Abdul Mejid died of tuberculosis, exactly as had his father, but others suggest his over-indulgent lifestyle was the cause. In her memoir, Marionca argues that Abdul Mejid's sly enemies had induced him into alcoholism, and that he simply drank himself to death. Given her expressed admiration for Abdul Mejid, her version cannot be ruled out.

Abdul Mejid was still alive and well during Evelina's years in Constantinople, and his sultanate was her background. For well over a dozen years Evelina had lived in convent schools in Rome. In 1849, when her father was well established as court physician and Abdul Mejid was on the throne, she found herself at home in the Constantinople she had left as a child of five.

One family version has it that initially Evelina and her two brothers—she was by then eighteen, Frederick sixteen, and the youngest, James, thirteen—were placed in a harem for safekeeping, just as they had been placed into a convent in Rome. This may have been true briefly even though boys normally left the harem—that is, the female quarters of a large family establishment—at age eleven, to be taught at home by a tutor. Instead the boys were put to board in a military school, Valata Serai.

As for Evelina, she was too old and too independent minded to live in the total seclusion of a harem, and there is no evidence that she did so. At eighteen it would have been assumed that her education was complete. Her stepbrother recalled that she was introduced into Pera society at the parties and balls organized by the diplomatic missions.

Even with the boys in military school, there were times when they returned home, and the entire family converged in the house, which, including its rash of servants, had become an amazingly large establishment. Not all was smooth sailing. One day, according to Frederick, they had been in Pera a year or so when Aunt Cornelia allowed a priest to visit the home. On learning of the priest's visit, her doctor brother Julius flew into the sort of uncontrolled rage which Marionca had described when she and Julius were first married.

"My house is not to be a nest of priests and Jesuits!" Julius shouted, as recorded by Frederick. Julius's indignation at what he saw as Catholic interference would have been aggravated both by his revived loyalty to his father and by the strict Protestantism of his third wife. According to Frederick, the scene Julius made about the priest's visit was no more than a "pretext," since his father had already wearied of Cornelia's presence. He ordered her to leave Constantinople on the first possible boat. Never mind that Cornelia had affectionately and conscientiously tended to Evelina and her brothers as they were growing up in Rome, as the thirteen years of her frequent, courteous, and generous letters to the then distant Julius show. One can only imagine the children's tears and Evelina's pained reaction.

As for her brothers, the two were taken by caique to the Beilerbey Palace, home of the Valide Sultan, who was temporarily absent, and installed in quarters there "under the care of a servant and some eunuchs" for almost a week. Upon her return, the Valide gave each boy a little golden purse, and on May 8, 1849, the boys were taken for a stay in the northwestern city of Yalova, 25 miles distant by ferryboat.

However traumatic, there are countless indications that Evelina nevertheless enjoyed Constantinople and adapted smoothly to its ways, never renouncing the Turkish portion of her heritage, while obviously taking pleasure in the cosmopolitan world of Pera. The French Catholic convent in which Evelina had been schooled and boarded in Rome had restricted her life to a limited number of contacts. Through her grandmother, the aging former lady-in-waiting to a Spanish royal, Evelina would have enjoyed some familiarity with the small circle of Spanish nobles living in the Eternal city, and with a few in the Italian papal nobility, particularly the Odescalchi. However, by the time Evelina was in her teens, her grandmother was increasingly impoverished, old, and ill. Nor would her maiden aunt Cornelia have had a large Roman circle.

Life in Pera had become far brighter and more challenging. Through her father, Evelina circulated within the British community, and, because she spoke Italian and French as well as English, within those communities as well. Pera was the scene of embassy parties and balls, which required that ball gowns be made by Turkish dressmakers—her first ball gowns ever.

Through the Valide Sultan, Evelina also had entree into the sultan's palace, where she would have enjoyed friendly contact with the women there. If this was a time when a degree of disappointment in the industrial revolution was causing intellectual Westerners to ask if the East might have more humane answers, the economic troubles of the Ottoman Empire were fostering interest in the West, as Esma and her brother's interest demonstrated. The harem women themselves were immensely curious about Western women, as the Western women diarists and travel writers have confirmed. After her visit to a harem, the English novelist and travel writer Isabella Frances Romer

wrote in 1849 that the women were fascinated at sight of this female outsider.
They were particularly struck at sight of Isabella's body when they realized
that it was constricted within a corset.

> In rising to make my adieu, my shawl fell off, and the three wives, in
> astonishment at the shape of my dress, so unlike their own, which leaves
> the waist quite unconfined, and everything else—To rise and fall as Heaven
> pleases, spanned round with their hands, and inquired how I could have got
> into my gown![16]

Once he was back in Constantinople, Evelina's ever unruly brother
Frederick learned that his mother was not in Paris, but in Turkey, and decided
that, when he was old enough, he would somehow track her down. In fact,
when he eventually learned just what had befallen his mother, and why she
was in Turkey, he made it his mission to find her.

What he discovered of Marionca's story was almost unbelievably painful and
dramatic. All had gone well during her first years of marriage to the ambitious
and able naval attaché Kibrizli. The couple had two children, a little girl and an
infant brother, and lived in a rather grand apartment. However, Kibrizli lost his
government post, and the family were forced to move into poor quarters, with
almost no furniture. Marionca herself related that money became so tight that
Kibrizli would hide indoors to dodge creditors pounding at the door.

After two years of misery, the situation turned around. In 1843, just when
Julius was basking in the friendship of the young sultan and his mother,
Kibrizli was dispatched to represent the government of Abdul Mejid at Akiah,
a fortified port near Jerusalem. Marionca joined him there and accompanied
her husband to Jerusalem, when Kibrizli was made its governor. By then
Marionca was 34; Evelina, who was still in Rome at that time, was fifteen.

Career advances continued, ever more rapidly. In 1848, Kibrizli was made
the sultan's envoy (ambassador, that is) to Belgrade.

In the meantime, the couple's first male child, Moharem-Bey, had died, but
then Marionca gave birth to another boy they named Djehad-Bey. The child
was born in 1848, the year when revolution swept the pope from Rome, to
flee for his safety into a fortress at Gaeta near Naples; that same revolutionary
fervor was what had permitted Julius to descend upon Rome in order to free
his children from the yoke of the Vatican. With the birth of a boy and the
career successes of her husband, Marionca's joy was boundless.

That joy soon came to a screeching halt. The family had been in Belgrade
less than a year when Kibrizli was again promoted, this time to the very
important and delicate post of Ottoman ambassador to the court of St. James
in London. According to Marionca, this latest triumph had come about
because she had been her husband's personal emissary to the sultan Abdul

Mejid. The Crimean War, which would break out in 1853 with the Ottomans allied with Britain, France, and Sardinia against Russia, was bubbling up, and Kibrizli's brief in England was to win support for Turkey from the cabinet of Henry Temple, the Viscount Palmerston, in its dealings with Russia.

The problem was that Kibrizli's posting to London meant that Marionca could not go there with him. No Muslim wife could accompany her husband to a non-Muslim state in which men could gaze upon her unveiled face—at least so Marionca was led to believe, presumably by Kibrizli himself.

Disaster struck shortly after Kibrizli had left for London. Marionca was alone when their new baby boy fell ill. Having lost one male child already, Marionca feared he too would die. Desiring to keep her husband from acquiring a fertile new wife who would give him another son, panicky Marionca did not turn a deaf ear when their Syrian housekeeper, Fatmah, whispered to her a clever solution.

"Well, madam," said Fatmah (in Marionca's own account), "you have only to buy a child of some unhappy creature, and to put him in the place of your own. The Pasha's absence affords a golden opportunity, which should not be lost."[17] Marionca was simply to feign pregnancy and then buy another woman's male child to keep as a reserve in case little Djehad-Bey died.

Marionca agreed. At her age, the biological clock was ticking loudly.

> The phantom of that [first] child's death … seemed to be pursuing me, and the dread I entertained of a catastrophe, so utterly blinded me that I believed everything to be possible. … It appeared to me that nothing could be easier than to give oneself out to be *enceinte*, and to borrow an infant, just as one may borrow a costume, or set of jewels.

To this end, the helpful housekeeper, Fatmah, consulted one of the family's eunuchs, Beshir. The boy babe was found, and Beshir helped by bringing him to the house. But then the real troubles began. The newly empowered housekeeper and eunuch together decided to up the ante by taking over rule of the household and of Marionca herself. Marionca could take their arrogance only so long and, in the end, infuriated, she retaliated by driving the housekeeper away.

However, she then made another mistake. Having firing Fatmah, she allowed Beshir to remain in the household. It was a literally fatal error, for when Fatmah learned that Beshir was still employed, she and her male accomplice, Omer ("her lover"), stole into the house just when Marionca was holding a reception in honor of her daughter's first reading of the Koran. Among the host of guests in attendance, none was aware when Fatmah and Beshir smothered the eunuch in the bathroom of the harem. The murder was cruel, for Fatmah suffocated Beshir with her buttocks over his face: "Such was Fatmah's rage against her victim, that she resolutely took his life herself, by sitting on his face, while Omer contented himself by throwing him down, and holding his hands."

But Beshir the eunuch had friends, and they reacted by breaking into the party and screaming, "Murder, murder! Vengeance!" Needless to say, the party was over.

For Marionca it most definitely was. For four months, she was held prisoner, albeit not in any common prison, but in a house. Those in power who had befriended her in Stamboul, and who had backed her husband's rapid promotions, were also compromised. On the other hand, among those Marionca believed rejoiced over her disgrace was none other than the powerful Esma, Abdul Mejid's mother and Julius's close friend in the sultan's palace.

In 1849, when Frederick was seventeen and newly arrived in Stamboul, Marionca was put on trial and accused by Fatmah and Omer of having ordered Beshir's murder. She was found guilty, but—since she was not the murderer—was punished by five years of banishment to Konya in Asia Minor, a city of 35,000 that lay some 435 miles distant from Constantinople. All her money and jewelry were confiscated.

Ambassador Kibrizli's friends—again, from Marionca's version—advised him that, to salvage his career, he needed to distance himself from his wife. The wisest course was therefore to divorce her and remarry as soon as possible. Taking their sage advice, Ambassador Kibrizli abandoned Marionca to her fate, and went on to become Grand Vizier (the equivalent of prime minister) of the Ottoman Empire in May of 1854.

All this Frederick would put together only later. When Frederick was eighteen, his father shipped him off to a boarding school in Scotland. He had been there only one year when, through friends of his father, he obtained a job at the Turkish Embassy in London, where Kibrizli had served as the Ottoman envoy. It was apparently while Frederick was working at the embassy that he learned the deeply disturbing news of his mother's plight and disgrace—that she had been put on trial as an accessory to a murder, convicted, imprisoned, and then sent into exile somewhere in Turkey.

It was too much to tolerate without action. In late 1851, Frederick made the decision to trace his mother, and to this end quit his London job to return to Turkey. His work at the embassy had given him names of people to contact, and in Constantinople, as resourceful as he was unruly, he wangled his way into the office of the War Minister, Mehemet Ali Pasha, to whom he appealed for help. When Ali Pasha told Frederick that his mother was living alone and in exile in faraway Konya, Frederick declared that he must go to visit her there. The minister, Frederick wrote later, not only arranged for him to have the necessary travel visa, but also gave him 30 pounds "out of his private purse" to pay for the 280-mile journey.[18] It is safe to say that Julius knew nothing of this adventure until afterward, for had he known, Julius would have blocked his son.

Marionca was visiting the home of a friend when she heard a knock on the door.

"All at once [I] saw an elegant looking young man, dressed in uniform, who suddenly walked into the room and up to the place where I was sitting. This strange apparition, and the boldness shown by the youth alarmed me."

But then the stranger threw his arms around her neck and cried out, "Don't you know me, mother? I am Frederick."

When he learned of it, Julius cannot have been pleased at this escapade, and may even have feared that Marionca would come to Constantinople (in fact, she would). Frederick, moreover, remained in touch with his mother over time and arranged to meet Kibrizli too, who "received him as a son," according to Frederick himself, in a pamphlet with anti-Semitic overtones written when he was 62, *Chasse à l'Homme* (De Gandini: Nice, 1894) (now in the Bibliotheque Nationale, Paris).[19] Claiming that Kibrizli had wanted to adopt him, he signed this book Osman Bey Kibrizli-Zade, although, after adventures in the Russian army, he had used yet another pseudonym for a time, Alexander Andrejevitch.

The story of father and wayward son did not end even there. Frederick later married and had a child, but he abandoned both. The child was given over to his father, Julius, and to Adelaide to care for—another addition to their large household.

Not long after her son dropped in to visit her at Konya, the ever undaunted Marionca took it upon herself to steal away from her exile in Konya to return to Constantinople. It is inconceivable that news of his first wife's return to the city where Julius and his family lived did not reach him.

But even then, during the final months of Evelina's life in Constantinople, the paths of mother and daughter did not cross, as Marionca acknowledged: "Since my marriage with Kibrizli-Pasha I had entirely lost sight of these dear children."[20] Instead Marionca became ever more involved in the complicated destiny of her second daughter, Aisha, who was born in 1842 and was around ten years old.

Having dumped Marionca, the ambitious Kibrizli had swiftly remarried. Aisha was living with her new stepmother in Constantinople while Kibrizli remained in London. The new wife took a dislike to the child born of Marionca and kept Aisha an unwilling, uneducated, and solitary prisoner in her father's house. A few years later, Aisha, still little more than a child, was married against her will to the teenaged son of Kibrizli's present wife, born of her previous marriage.

Just as the official version lingers that Julius murdered Lord Byron, the official van Millingen version was, and is, that from the outset Marionca was mad as a hatter—"depraved," was the word used by Julius's stepson, J. R. van Millingen, in his family chronicle. It was preferred not to take into account that at age seventeen or so Marionca had been irresponsibly seduced by a man of thirty and removed from the only, very limited world she had ever known in Galata.

Nor does this version take into account that, after being banished in Rome from Julius's mother's version of Christian society, Marionca retreated, and for a decade with relative success, into Muslim Stamboul. She changed her name and became a Muslim herself before learning to what extent the women were kept literal captives and even casually murdered when they broke ranks.

At this point, it is fair to inquire about the nature of harems. Before Kibrizli divorced her, Marionca had herself lived for a time in a harem. Evelina, who had learned to speak some Turkish, visited the palace harem at Topkapi, and her father Julius earned at least some of his keep there.

The fact is that there were two harems. The first was that imagined by men, who had no possibility of actually seeing it; even Julius, if he were able to visit his protector, the aging Valide Sultan, in her quarters, could not have seen the harem, for Esma had her own courtyard with outside access and her own two-story apartment with a large staff. The harem staff was far larger still, which began with its teams of black and white eunuchs who guarded the women (and amused them and occasionally made love to them). Esma was the efficient manager of this vast operation in the same way its manager runs a hotel.

At the same time, the mid-nineteenth century harem was also a fantasy vogue of European artists and writers. Lady Mary Wortley Montagu, wife of the British ambassador to Turkey, had made a number of visits to the harem in the mid-eighteenth century. Her *Letters and Works,* published long after her death in 1837, describes that part of the harem she was able to visit and offers a sketchy view of the lives of the women there. The women, she wrote, were:

> ... the only women in the world that lead a life of uninterrupted pleasure exempt from cares; the whole time being spent in visiting, bathing, or in the agreeable amusement of spending money, and inventing new fashions.[21]

"A life of uninterrupted pleasure": whether correct or not (and her descriptions were challenged by other women writers, including Emmeline Lott in *Harem Life in Egypt and Constantinople,* published in 1866), her words evoke Oriental beauties lounging about the harem. These evocations inspired male artists like Ingres to paint harem scenes redolent of erotic content which was derived solely from their own imaginings.

Another tourist who fostered the image of the hyper-sexualized Oriental woman was French writer Gustave Flaubert, then 27, after meeting and having sex with a beautiful dancer and courtesan named Kuchu-Hanem in a town called Esna in Upper Egypt. In March of 1850, and again in April of 1851, Flaubert reveled in the two nights he spent with her, and later described her sexual charms in plain, anatomical terms. These charms became all the more notoriously popular when other mid-Victorian Western writers evoked them in their own ecstatic writings.

But no one had more lingering effects upon male Western daydream celebrations of the harem than the proto-porno novel *The Lustful Turk, or Scenes in the Harem of an Eastern Potentate*, published by an anonymous male in English in 1828.[22] The date is important: by then mechanical printing of paper had made mass publishing possible, and books were being sold in railway stations to the English public, literate since the previous century because of the Protestant insistence upon reading the Bible. In this epistolary novel, a nice English young woman traveler to Algiers named Emily exchanges letters with her friend Sylvia back home. All begins well, but then Emily is raped by North African pirates, and after she becomes the slave of "The Dey," who speaks Turkish, she loves the sex. "He withdrew his hand from between my thighs, forced me on my back on the couch, and in an instant turned up my clothes above my navel. … Exhausted as I was and lost in desire, I could make no further resistance." And so forth and so on until Emily lets herself go, in lingering detail, lapsing happily into "the tumult of my senses." Never mind that later a maid is bound, flogged, and raped.

What is curious about this early harem pornography is that it has borrowings from Byron: "The Dey himself [is] a Byronic figure," writes Steven Marcus in *The Other Victorians: a study of Sexuality and Pornography in mid-nineteenth-Century England*.[23] The lascivious harem figures in Byron's Canto 5 of *Don Juan*. In the slave market, Juan is sold to a black eunuch named Baba from the harem. Threatened by Baba with castration unless he agrees to dress as a woman, Juan is obliged to meet the sultan's beautiful most recent wife who, it turns out, had spotted Juan in the market and had persuaded Baba to buy him. (Loving another, Juan refuses her advances.)

The effects of *The Lustful Turk* went well beyond the nineteenth century and into the next. As Hsu-Mig Teo writes in his essay "Orientalism and mass market romance novels in the twentieth century," *The Lustful Turk* was pioneer pornography which "outsourced" sex to the Orient while punishing white European "ladies" for their chastity and coldness, all because the European code of chivalry had emasculated European men.[24]

More subtle with the Victorians but also influential was the poetic, exuberant exoticism of the love tales in *The Arabian Nights*, in translation in Europe after 1704. Even the European artists' popular street scenes of

Constantinople and Cairo were allusions to the enticements of the harem, for in showing veiled women, the paintings "inevitably alluded to the private space of the harem in which those veils could be removed and from which all men except the master of the household were excluded ... the veil was like an extension of the harem."[25] At a certain point, such was the popularity of the harem, perhaps echoing a degree of momentary envy, that Ottoman-style masked balls were held in mid-nineteenth century England, with the proper English ladies dressed in what they believed were harem fashions.

If these were all eroticizing fantasy harems, Marionca was a woman who lived in a real harem for three decades (according to her account), and found it remarkably boring, save for the chitchat with the eunuchs who were its guards. Later Marionca would be forced to realize that her life had been at grave risk at various times, and that she too could have been chopped apart and the bits put to float in the Bosphorus. The same could have happened to Aisha, Evelina's half-sister.

It took some years, but Marionca finally rescued Aisha from her harem captivity within a miserable marriage. After various vicissitudes, the two would manage to flee to Paris. There, having no income and needing to earn survival money, Marionca took advantage of the era's anti-slavery sentiment, combined with the Europeans' sensationalistic fascination with the harem, to write about her life. Her book, *Thirty Years in the Harem* (1872), was originally published in French and then translated into English. Co-author of its sequel, *Six Years in Europe*, published the following year, was the noted anti-slavery activist and author, Louis Alexis Chamerovzow, who very probably was responsible for a good part of *Thirty Years*.

In the end, Marionca, despite or because of her tortured life, told what appeared to be the real story, and today her book remains a useful contribution to the literature of the harem. On the other hand, it is curious that the book appeared, and to success in Europe, exactly at the time when women in Ottoman Turkey were being emancipated in what today's scholars know as the Tanzimat era, which after 1839 brought the Ottomans closer to Europe and ushered in reforms concerning women, including their education and property rights.

For her already Westernized, Catholic daughter, Evelina, the harem held few charms. Approaching 20 years of age, she was already appearing to be an old maid—or was, until she was suddenly swept away from Constantinople and the Ottoman world.

5

Escapade

While living in Pera and visiting across the river in Stamboul during the crucial years of her emerging adulthood, Evelina had no reason to believe that she would ever leave that new home, where she had, apparently happily, rediscovered the fascinating father she had lost so many years before. Despite her father's dozen years of absence from Rome, his disastrous quarrel with Evelina's mother, the rarity of his letters to Evelina, his failure to send funds for the upkeep of his three children, and, most recently, his banishing her loving aunt Cornelia from his household in Pera, Evelina worshipped her father: he was "the most passionate affection" of her youth, as she confided to a close friend many years later. Thus, Evelina immersed herself in her new life and learned to love Constantinople and its culture.

Not every observer saw it that way. Her troublesome but not unintelligent brother Frederick, who was observing Evelina at first hand, was convinced that his sister disliked Constantinople and its ways, but that since childhood she had been accustomed to concealing her true feelings. She had acquired this trait in Rome, he believed, because her two younger brothers had been petted and pampered by their grandmother and aunt, whereas Evelina, pretty but painfully shy, had been left to tend to herself and to keep her own counsel.

That darkness existed in her background. In Rome, Evelina had been without a father for twelve years, and motherless since she was six years old. As a child, she had witnessed the battles between her disturbed and alienated mother and her maniacal grandmother. She had seen her mother collapse into a self-confessed nervous breakdown and then be cast out of Palazzo Odescalchi—just where, the child could not know or imagine. Then the adolescent Evelina had been a bystander watching the vicious campaign waged by her father and grandfather against her aging and ever weaker grandmother, whose response was always to say she would pray for her son.

In Constantinople, if not from her father, gossip about Evelina's mother might have been passed on to her by servants in the big house loyal to Adele, or by the women she met during Evelina's occasional visits to the harem in Stamboul. It could hardly be a secret that, just when Evelina was eighteen and newly arrived in Pera, Marionca had been involved in the murder of a eunuch in 1848, and for this had been put on trial and then banished to distant Konya. Her brother, Frederick, at least, managed to learn this and was not one to keep a secret.

Nor were Evelina's Pera years eased by her stepmother's Protestant severity, which must have sorely tested Evelina's Catholicism. Her home life was doubtless further aggravated by the fact that her stepmother and father set out to find suitors who might marry her.

Such a turbulent background would either break a sensitive child or turn her into steel. Evelina became steel—albeit veiled steel—and adapted to Pera just as she had adapted to Rome. At the same time that life inside the Roman convent atop the Spanish Steps was strict, the French nuns of the Sacred Heart who had taught and housed her were not stupid. However narrow their experience, they had taught her to speak and to write correctly in at least three languages, English, Italian, and French. And they had taught her self-discipline.

It did not hurt Evelina's marital prospects that, as her photographs show, she was slender and remarkably pretty, with dark hair and bright eyes. But engaging looks would not have been enough. Through the vicissitudes of her childhood in Rome, Evelina had learned to be resourceful. She was resilient enough to seek out and to find the positive side of her life in Constantinople. During her five years there she absorbed the ways of that other world, so utterly different from Catholic Rome. She made friends inside the sultan's harem and learned to enjoy dressing in Turkish clothing.

In 1850, when Evelina was nineteen years old, she already frequented the "aristocratic" diplomatic families living in Pera, as Frederick confirms. In particular, she was befriended by a charming and extraordinarily sophisticated older woman, the childless wife of a diplomat, the French-born Countess Ermance-Catherine de Boutet de Sturmer. This was the great friendship of Evelina's life. In Pera, two years older than Evelina's father, Ermance became a unique role model for Evelina even as the motherless young woman became the surrogate daughter of the gifted, experienced Ermance.

Born February 25, 1798, Ermance was the daughter of a War Ministry official in Paris, where, at age seventeen, she met and married a twenty-nine-year-old junior diplomat from Austria of Hungarian descent. Bartholomaus von Sturmer (usually called, as if in French, Barthelemi de Sturmer) happened to have been born in 1787 in Pera, where his father, a baron, was serving as Austrian ambassador.

With her husband, the new bride Ermance had traveled to Sainte-Hélène in 1816, where Sturmer had been charged by Austrian Chancellor Prince Klemens von Metternich with what amounted to espionage duties. Metternich warned Sturmer that he was to have no direct contact with Napoleon, but was to write a monthly report on him and to be on the alert for any attempt on the part of the exiled emperor to flee from the island; the previous year, Napoleon had successfully escaped from Elba. In one of Sturmer's obligatory reports (now part of the Napoleonic oeuvre and published in 1887), he avowed that, "Bonaparte eats a lot, puts on fat and does no exercise ... One sees him too rarely walking on foot in front of his house." In March of 1818, Sturmer wrote that Napoleon had been suffering from heart palpitations, severe enough to "oblige him to remain standing" upright all night. His face was wan, his skin yellowed with jaundice, his eyes blank.

Napoleon seems to have desired to meet Sturmer, but neither the Austrians nor the English would allow it, the latter considering Sturmer a spy. Moreover, his Parisian wife, Ermance, was suspected of being a Napoleon sympathizer and of attempting to arrange secret contact with him. As a result, never once did Sturmer have any contact with Napoleon during the two years of his stay on the island. This "thankless and painful mission" left Sturmer frustrated and miserable, he wrote to Metternich in Vienna, adding significantly, if undiplomatically, that, "Without such a companion [Ermance], the melancholy would already have weighed heavily on me, and I would not have been able to reach the end of my tour. ... She enriches my existence."[2]

The tour of duty at Sainte-Hélène ended that same year, 1818, and Sturmer was appointed Austria's first envoy to the United States. Austria did not yet recognize the U.S., so it was planned for his arrival to coincide with official recognition of the young American nation. But shortly before their scheduled departure, Ermance fell ill, and her husband had to write Metternich to decline the appointment (in fact, it was merely postponed). As a result, as Sir Adolphus Slade (1804-1877), the Englishman who served as Vice-Admiral in the Turkish navy, wrote in 1839, because of Ermance's illness, the Austrian cabinet "abandoned its intention of accrediting a minister to the President, nor was one sent to Washington until 1838. ... The indisposition of a fair lady caused the formal recognition of a great state to be delayed for twenty years!"[3]

What "indisposition?" A grave miscarriage is the first thought that comes to mind, for, although Sturmer and Ermance had a grandnephew who became a close friend of Rasputin in Russia, the Sturmers would have no children of their own.

Later that year the couple were able to begin their American tour of duty, stationed in Philadelphia. Then came a posting to Rio de Janeiro before they were finally able to withdraw into the elegance of Habsburg, Vienna.

This was the gilded "Age of Metternich," and for several years the couple circulated in Viennese high society, all music, grand balls, sumptuous banquets, wild boar hunts, parties with fireworks, festive jousts, gallant men, and fashionable women (like the dozens with whom Metternich notoriously had affairs).

By then a full-fledged socialite, Ermance was also an intelligent woman who found time to correspond in French with a "Madame Montagu" (probably the Marquise de Montagu, Anne-Paule-Dominique de Noailles, the noteworthy sister of Lafayette's wife); their exchange of letters was of sufficient interest that it was later published in England. During their Vienna years, the sophisticated, well-traveled Ermance became a particular friend of Metternich's teenaged daughter Princess Leontine. One of his thirteen acknowledged children, Leontine would marry the Hungarian Count Moritz Sandor in 1835. But during the years while the Sturmers were in Vienna, Leontine was still unwed, and the friendship between the older and childless Ermance Sturmer and the much younger girl was a prelude to Ermance's relationship with Evelina.

From Vienna, Sturmer, exactly like his father, was made ambassador to Constantinople, and in 1832 returned to the city where he was born—Pera.

Sturmer's tour of duty coincided with that of the famous English ambassador John Ponsonby, 1st Viscount Ponsby (1770-1755). Everyone in Pera knew everyone else, and the Sturmers were quickly inserted into the diplomatic social whirl of Pera, which gravitated inevitably around Ponsonby. Vice-Admiral Slade left a vivid description of the Sturmers' position: "Pera boasted of very good society," Slade wrote, and in this "very good society" Sturmer was one of the town's four "kings." The Sturmer parties brought together diplomats from England, Russia, Prussia, Sweden, Greece, Spain, Sardinia, and Florence.

The observant Vice-Admiral Slade is himself of some interest. For seventeen years, he served as administrative chief of the Turkish Navy, where he was known as Muchaver Pasha. Although he could not enter into the harem proper, at one point Slade became one of the few allowed to walk beyond the Gate of Felicity into the semi-public rooms of the Seraglio: its Library, Throne Room, Divan (parlor), and kitchens, where he saw "not less than a hundred dinners were preparing, each at a yawning cavern of flames and smoke that might have graced Vulcan's workshop."[4]

"We might occasionally meet them [the other diplomats] at the Baron de Sturmer's, whose house was the only 'open' one," wrote Sturmer. "With the men came their ladies." His wife Ermance was very "accomplished," entertaining at her parties with her fine singing voice.[5] (In fact, it was Count Sturmer; his father was the baron.)

Slade knew the Sturmers well, for at one point he had taken a boat trip down the Danube together with Sturmer and "his accomplished lady." Theirs was a cosmopolitan world, and others on board included the English Mr. Isfording (who was Sturmer's attaché) and two American travelers, Mr. Littlefield, and his ward, Miss Holmes.

Sturmer's days as a suspected Austrian spy were thus long forgotten, and in Pera, Sturmer, fluent in English thanks to his ambassadorship in the United

States, was noted as particularly friendly and hospitable with the English speakers. "Baron Sturmer is known to most Englishmen visiting Pera, by his hospitality and by his attention to the English, to whom, from circumstances, he is much attached," wrote Slade. "It would be difficult to meet with a more accomplished and amiable couple than the Baron and his lady (a Parisian)."[6]

Indeed they were amiable, in part because their marriage was particularly happy, as is revealed by Sturmer's writing, "We were made for each other. Never was a union happier than ours."

Sturmer finally retired from the diplomatic service in 1850, and the couple left Pera to live in Venice, still ruled by his native Austria. By that time, the grand days of the Venetian Republic were long gone, and the industrial age had left Venice behind. The city of Venice had become a literal backwater—a local transit port, "marginal in the Mediterranean for geo-political reasons," in large part thanks to Austrian rule of the Veneto following the defeat of Napoleon, according to the economic historian Adolfo Bernardello.

This poverty of Venice explains why, in 1852, two years after their retirement in Venice, the Sturmers were not hard pressed to purchase the literally palatial Palazzo Coccina-Tiepolo, midway between the Rialto and the Accademia Bridges. Overlooking the Grand Canal, it was built in the late sixteenth century by the wealthy Coccina family of Bergamo; the following century, Tiepolo decorated the ceiling of its great hall.

This, then, was the unabashedly romantic couple who showed Evelina another existence which she could idealize. Ermance—worldly, hospitable, loving, and deeply loved by her husband—was one of the first, if not the first, interesting, exciting, cultivated, and fulfilled woman whom Evelina had ever known, and known intimately. Before Ermance, there had been the nuns of the convent in which Evelina was boarded. There had been her maiden aunt and feisty grandmother. There was, in Pera, her pious Protestant stepmother, who was also the busy stepmother to a half-dozen other children. And somewhere out there, cast out from a harem, was her murderous mother. The Sturmers, moreover, enjoyed the happiest marriage Evelina had ever been able to observe. Their lives were Evelina's university education, they were her models, their parties and hospitality and cosmopolitan friends hers, their life the one she longed to live.

Having taken Evelina under her wing in Pera, Ermance wrote Evelina inviting her to visit them in Venice.

There is no way Evelina could travel alone by packet. Her father was unable or preferred not to accompany her, but the Sturmers had carefully arranged that she be accompanied by the wife of one of Sturmer's colleagues from the Austrian embassy in Constantinople, a Mme. Ros (presumably short for Roswitha) Steindl. Ros's husband was a mid-level diplomat who, following a tour of duty in Jaffa, had served under Ambassador Sturmer.

But first Julius had to agree. There were many arguments in favor of allowing Evelina this adventure. Julius can hardly have failed to be concerned that, at age 21, Evelina was, by Constantinople standards and by those of his wife as well, practically "the last grape on the vine," as the Victorian-era phrase went, who risked becoming an old maid like her aunt Cornelia. Marriage for a young woman was at the top of most family agendas in that and many other eras, and Julius may have agreed, in the end, hoping to place Evelina upon the marriage market in Europe, Pera having turned up no suitor acceptable to her after almost four years.

Her brother Frederick held that Evelina herself longed to escape into marriage, but had snubbed the local horde at Constantinople even as her father and stepmother sought suitors for her. As Frederick wrote, "From the day of our arrival Evelina was resolved to emancipate herself from her emancipator and to go out to find a marriage nicely far from him [Julius]. This resolution was executed later by her with consummate art and finesse."

Another possible motive for Julius's agreeing to allow his daughter to travel to Europe with Mme. Steindl was fear. Fully aware that Marionca was in Konya, Julius may have been concerned that his mad former wife might descend upon their home and their daughter; in fact, Marionca would shortly quit Konya and return to Constantinople, not for Evelina's sake, but to reclaim her other daughter, the younger Aisha, Evelina's half-sister and the daughter of Kibrizli.

But there is also a family version. By that account, from Rome, Aunt Cornelia had become a matchmaker, arranging for Evelina to meet and to marry a certain well-born Venetian gentleman. This was based upon two difficult assumptions: first, that somehow the spinster aunt had well-placed contacts in Venice, and, second, that somehow—and this appeared unlikely, after Julius had evicted Cornelia from his home in Pera—Cornelia and her brother Julius were again on friendly terms.

Packing her bag, Evelina had carefully and proudly placed in it her finest Turkish gown, to be put into service for eventual grand parties. Doubtless, in the Pera household filled with children, there was little money for having a European-style gown made for her (although these were beginning to be popular with the upper crust in the harem). In Pera there were dressmakers who turned out Greek-style outfits for the Greek community, but this was not for Evelina. Nor would it have been easy to manufacture the era's famous obligatory corset to be worn beneath a European-style gown, with crinoline and hour-glass waist.

On the contrary, for literally decades Evelina would persist obstinately and proudly in dressing Turkish style for great occasions, and donned Turkish dress while posing for at least two formal portraits. In Venice, she would sometimes be called by the Venetian women aristocrats, with a hint of disregard, "La Turchesina" (the Little Turk). To borrow a term coined by sociologists, hers was "cultural cross dressing," and it involved her very identity.[7]

She and Mme. Ros Steindl had barely entered the great Grand Canal palazzo as the Sturmers' guests when they were told that they were to dress for the evening at the opera. Evelina prepared herself for the musical performance, and for her own introductory performance in Venetian society, by wearing her best Turkish gown.

What Evelina entered that evening was not the original La Fenice Theater built in 1792. True to its name, which means "The Phoenix," the theater had burned down in 1836 and was reborn, entirely reconstructed ten months later. Once again, its great doorways opened onto such a small piazza that to come upon the opera house was, and is, something of a surprise. Behind is another important entrance, which has its own tiny canal port, where parties of opera-goers, including the Sturmers and their guests from Constantinople, arrived by private gondola.

This was the great season for Italian grand opera, and around that time Rossini, Bellini, and Donizetti were all mounting operas on the stage of La Fenice. In the months to come Evelina would see a variety of theirs, but that first night it is likely that she attended a performance of an opera by Giuseppe Verdi, whose newest works, beginning in 1844, were regularly presented at La Fenice. For many of the performances, Verdi personally oversaw the rehearsals at La Fenice, which included, in 1853, both "Il Trovatore" and "La Traviata." Later Richard Wagner would also come to Venice, where he wrote Act II of Tristan and Isolde.

Inside the opera theater, before the candle lights were quenched, Evelina caused a sensation in her exotic Turkish outfit. Although she would not have realized it, the vision of a handsome woman dressed *à la Turque* inevitably evoked those male fantasy harem images that had made their way into the European paintings and literature of that period. Her gown was an enhancement of the charms of an already beautiful and elegant young woman, but it also made Evelina the embodiment of that fantasy harem of the European male imagination. This was all the more true of Venice, with its ancient ties to Constantinople.

If she were seen, it was because she and her friend were in the box maintained by Count and Countess Sturmer. But because the Sturmers moved among Austrian friends and the diplomatic circles in Venice, her introduction to the 37-year-old Count Almorò III Giovanni Giuseppe Pisani (known familiarly as Almorò) may have come via other, Italian channels. Exactly which channels, whether her aunt was involved or not, exactly where the two met, who introduced them, and when—that, we do not know. What is known is that, after that introduction, Evelina and her chaperone Mme. Steindl lingered with the Sturmers in Venice for several months, and that by the end of that fairly brief lapse of time, the young spinster Evelina was formally betrothed to the more mature bachelor, Count Almorò Pisani.

Although they would know each other for several months, the newly engaged couple had little time to learn anything that was intimate about each other. Indeed it is doubtful that, before they were married, they were ever able to speak with each other without a chaperone. This is all the more true given the absence of Evelina's father; the risk of gossip or even scandal would have been too great, especially given Evelina's Turkish background.

Much later Evelina's brother Frederick, who made no effort to be kind, dismissed Almorò as possessing the two qualities one might most appreciate in a husband: "He was at one and the same time very rich and very stupid." As we shall see, Frederick was wrong on both counts. Almorò was neither stupid, nor rich. His title and property gave the Count the semblance of being extraordinarily wealthy, but the concept of "very rich" can be ambiguous, for it depends upon who's counting.

For most outsiders, Almorò would have been deemed a fine catch, and for his future bride, a trophy. The Pisani were among the most distinguished of all Venetian patrician families, and had left lasting traces upon their city and the entire Veneto region. In the early Middle Ages, fur traders came from Pisa to Venice once a year, then settled there permanently around the year 905. Among Almorò's distinguished ancestors was that Admiral Nicolò Pisani, who had triumphed over Genoa in 1324 in a naval battle for control of shipping lanes to the East. In the 1520s, one Pisani, Giovanni, served as ambassador from Venice to the court of the Medici pope Clement VII. Gradually the Pisani came to enjoy immense power in Venice, moving from trade into banking, and then diplomacy, the military, agriculture, politics, and the church; two Pisani became cardinals.

One of these was Cardinal Francesco Pisani, who commissioned in 1552 his architect friend, Andrea Palladio, to design a villa for him at the ancient town of Montagnana, north of Padua. Half town mansion, half country house, Palladio fitted into its neo-classical facade a fine double loggia, or two stories of inset, colonnaded balconies. The villa at Montagnana is now listed as a UNESCO World Heritage Site.

Besides the grand, showy villa at Montagnana, Cardinal Francesco had built a second Villa Pisani on fertile farmland at the little town of Vescovana in the flat Veneto mainland. Typical of the Republic's patrician families, this estate, despite the fact that agricultural production in the region was heavily conditioned by the climate, was important, for it produced income to flow into the family coffers.

In the centuries to come, multiple branches of the Pisani family continued to dwell in and near Venice, but of these, Evelina's fiancé Almorò was the very last direct descendant of the most famous and wealthy of all: the doge Alvise Pisani (1664-1741). Beginning as a prosecutor in Venice, Alvise became a diplomat, representing the Venetian Republic first to Austria, and then as ambassador to Spain and France. In January of 1735, when he was 71, he was elected doge of the Republic of Venice. From the Latin *dux,* the title implies military as well as political leadership. The Venetian economy had been in a recession, but under doge Alvise's stewardship, it flourished once more, thanks to the introduction onto its warships of a new and devastating battery of cannon.

Grandeur came naturally to Alvise, who seems to have loved making and spending money. As soon as he was elected doge he went to live in the Palazzo Ducale in the heart of Venice with his wife and two sons; one was named Luigi for the Sun King Louis XIV, who baptized the baby in the chapel at Versailles. Alvise enjoyed parties, including the costumed celebration of "Carnivale"— that Carnivale, or the pre-Lenten festivity of *Mardi Gras,* which to this day attracts thousands of visitors to Venice every year.

The doge Alvise's most lasting monument is the huge baroque Villa Pisani at Strà. Overlooking the Brenta Canal eighteen miles west of Venice, it had been designed in 1552 by Palladio for Cardinal Francesco Pisani, as we have seen. Now, in an elaborate show of Pisani power, Alvise had architect Francesco Maria Preti bring it to spectacular completion, enlarging it to have 114 rooms.

By that time, the Pisani were extravagantly rich, also through a marriage to an heiress of another patrician family from Venice, the Mocenigo. They did not hide their light under a bushel. When Alvise died after his six years as doge, his heirs decided to embellish further both the villa at Strà, and their own name, commissioning, in the early 1760s, Domenico Tiepolo to paint, high overhead on the ballroom ceiling of that villa, a vast fresco depicting "The Apotheosis [Glory] of the Pisani Family." (Less glorious was a meeting there between Adolf Hitler and Benito Mussolini in 1934. The painting is still in situ in what is today a national monument.)

In Venice itself, from the late 16th century onward, the Pisani had owned and resided in an enormous, four-story palace. Because it faced onto the Campo Santo Stefano, that particularly wealthy and powerful Pisani branch came to be known as the "Pisani da Santo Stefano." This was the branch into which Evelina married.

The principal land façade of Palazzo Pisani had been designed in the early seventeenth century by (it is believed) architect Bartolomeo Monopola, who had also designed the magnificent portico of the Doges's Palace. This was broad, facing onto the small square known as the Campiello Pisani (the Little Pisani Square). On the opposite side was a rather humble boat landing entrance, where gondolas could enter via a dark and spooky-looking narrow canal called the Calle di Portico Pisani.

Two monumental seventeenth century statue groups by Girolamo Campagna, representing the labors of Hercules, guarded a gateway to the palazzo at Campo Santo Stefano. And well they might guard the palazzo: as an inventory of 1809 showed, in it were 159 paintings by, among others, Titian, Tintoretto, Veronese, Lorenzo Lotto, Jacopo da Bassano, Paris Bordon, Anthony Van Dyck, and Palma il Vecchio. Many dated from the vibrant years of the Venetian sixteenth century. Inside the palazzo, in addition, were collections of rare coins and medals, and of books.

The mammoth palazzo of the Pisani da Santo Stefano was not flawless: it had no entrance from a canal nor windows overlooking water. A decade after the family doge died in 1741, the family spent 8,000 ducats to buy from a scientist named Marquis Giovanni Poleni an adjacent palazzo dating from the fourteenth century, whose narrow facade gave onto the Grand Canal. Located between Piazza San Marco and the bridge of the Accademia, it rose directly across the Grand Canal from the Church of the Salute. On its Grand Canal side, the new addition was fairly narrow, with just three bays. On the third floor was its piano *nobile*, where each of the twin bifora windows gave onto a balcony. So as to join it to their own vast palazzo, the Pisani simply broke through its rear wall. The new wing maintained its own personality, however, and, while the larger building was still known as the Palazzo Pisani, this new wing came to be called the Palazzetto Pisani.

In the late eighteenth century, Almorò Alvise Pisani (1754-1808), and his younger brother, our Almorò's father, Almorò Francesco Pisani (1759-1836), were the heirs to the doge and to the Campo Stefano family heritage. (Most confusingly for journalists like myself, and perhaps also for historians, any number of baby Pisani were named by greedy parents Almorò because, in the will he wrote in 1682, the wealthy prosecutor Almorò Pisani had made it a conceited condition that only heirs named Almorò could inherit family property.)

But times had changed. Despite the wealth inherited and wasted by previous generations, and despite the brothers carrying on the name "Almorò," by the time the two inherited the vestiges of the family fortunes, a devastating decline was in act. As their father had acknowledged in his will of 1740, he had enjoyed a position of manifest financial wealth in 1728, but then found himself in grave difficulty. He had gone deeply into debt, he explained, in order to pay for improvements to the villa at Strà and the palazzo in Venice. "Besides the sums needed for the buildings, to a great extent the need for commodious lodgings, pleasures and ornaments have all absorbed considerable of my funds," he admitted with devastating candor.[8]

Nevertheless, both his young heirs were irresponsible wastrels, whose foolishness aggravated an already difficult financial situation. In 1763, when he was appointed prosecutor of San Marco in Venice, the 20-something elder brother Almorò Alvise Pisani celebrated by having bread and wine handed out as a gift to the people of Venice. The two brothers then threw a party for their fellow aristocrats. The doge himself attended, wearing a Carnival-style mask which did not quite conceal his identity. Coffee was served in Japanese cups resting upon saucers of solid gold.

To celebrate the arrival of springtime in May of 1784, the brothers threw another fête in their summer retreat on the island of the Giudecca, the Casina Pisani, which they had enlarged for the occasion. Because spring had actually arrived late that year, they had the gardens decorated with faux trees enhanced with crystal blossoms and woven leaves. "Thousands" of real flowering plants were scattered about the grounds. By way of a grand entryway, they had a torch-lit arch of triumph erected. The cost: 17,700 ducats.

This was in the grand Pisani tradition of old. Two centuries before this, the rugged, militaristic King of Sweden, Gustavus Adolphus III, had come to Venice on a visit. To entertain him, the Pisani of that era had offered a ball attended by eight hundred guests. The tables were served by 170 servants, which were set with specially ordered plates of solid gold. Taking his leave, King Gustavus, who at that time vied with the pope in Rome as the most powerful ruler in Europe, confided that he would never be able to do anything similar back home in his gloomy castle in Stockholm.

The Venetian economy was gloomier still, suffering from its inability to compete with the new manufacturing industry developing on mainland North Italy, especially in Lombardy. Even as queen of the sea, Venice was in deep trouble, superseded, thanks to Austrian preference, by the port at Trieste, further to the north.

Despite this, Venice resisted renewal. At least one eighteenth century politician, the diplomat Andrea Tron (1712-1785), was cognizant of the risk that, lacking a work ethic, Venetian fortunes were destined to decline.[9] The son of a wool manufacturer and scion of one of the fine old patrician families, Tron complained that Venice was run by only two or three hundred families, who live "a soft life" of costly luxury. "Venice prospers, but its wealth does not produce other wealth; it devours that of others as a parasite, it offers nothing new," warned Tron.[10]

Corruption was widespread, and the city administration was antiquated and Byzantine, with such offices as "Executor against Swearing," "Quarantia Criminale" (a criminal court dating from around 1200), and "Comptroller of Superficial Expenditures," who presumably did no such thing.

Worse was to come. In 1797, after 1,000 years of independence, an invading Napoleon ousted the last doge, Ludovico Manin, and shut down the Venetian equivalent of a Parliament. Napoleon ceded Venice, along with Istria and Dalmatia, to Austria in the Treaty of Campo Formio. This was the fall of the Venetian Republic.

With Austria's help, it ushered in a deep recession. By 1813, when Napoleon's era was coming to an end, Venetians were starving. To survive, we are told, priests were reduced to selling off the altars of their churches. A terrible description of this newly impoverished Venice comes from Hester Lynch Thrale (formerly Mrs. Piozzi). Writing on July 26, 1815, she related that an acquaintance, the English poet Samuel Rogers, had just returned from Venice with heartbreaking news.

> The ancient Nobles Men and Women beg Charity in the public Streets—all Mirth and Gayety are banished. Madame Foscarini wore a thick Veil; but threw it up, acknowledging Rogers' Companion for an old Acquaintance: She held out her hand, They kissed and dropt Tears on it, and put a Small Coin in:—some who saw them shouted Viva l'Inglesi![11]

According to American historian Ronald S. Cunsolo, "By 1845, Austria took 45,000,000 Austrian lire more *from* the region than she spent [my italics]. By refusing to grant credit to progressive entrepreneurs, the slow, bungling Austrian bureaucracy impeded the growth of Venetian capitalism."[12]

Only three years after this, a popular insurrection against the Austrians swept the Veneto. Its leader, a brilliant lawyer named Daniele Manin, was made president of a provisional government on March 22, 1848. For Manin, the Austrians saw Venetians as living in "a mere outlying village of Vienna. [But] We ought to be governed according to our character and customs, and to have a true national representation and a moderately free press."

The Austrians arrested Manin in January 1848, but at this, the Venetians rebelled until their agitation brought Manin's release. A provisional government of the Venetian Republic was named, and Manin was declared its president that March. This defiance of Austrian authority led to war.

At the Marghera Fort (near Mestre, and today a public park), Manin's 2,500 troops were faced off against 30,000 Austrians under Field Marshall Count Joseph Radetzky. In the first aerial bombardment in history, Radetzky had bombs dropped from balloons onto the rebels. At the same time, a cholera epidemic broke out.

The revolution had failed. Manin fled into exile in Paris, and Austrian rule was re-established with the surrender of Venice on August 27.

The fortunes of the Pisani da Santo Stefano suffered along with the decline of the fortunes of their fellow Venetians. When their villa at Strà became too costly to maintain, they sold it in 1807 to Napoleon himself for 973,000 gold francs, or 1.9 million Venetian lire.

Three years later, the Pisani sold their collection of rare books and maps for 22,000 Italian lire; several of its maps dating from the fifteenth century are now owned by Stanford University. Next on the docket were the majority of the

Pisani collection of rare coins and medals. A large ceiling painting by Veronese showing Jove with Neptune was sold to the Kaiser-Friedrich-Museum in Berlin (now the Bode Museum), but destroyed in a bombing of 1945.[13] The Pisani's ballroom ceiling painting of "Aurora and the Air Nymphs," by Giovanni Antonio Pellegrini (1675-1741), considered a masterpiece, wound up in the 8,000-acre Biltmore Estate, in Ashville, North Carolina. Now a historic house museum, here the movie "Forrest Gump" was filmed.

Like the villa at Strà, the family's huge Palazzo Pisani had to be sold. The palace which had belonged to the Pisani is now empty, wrote Hester Piozzi (1741-1821) sorrowfully. "Tumbling to the pavement. ... its Possessors turned out to wander. ... What has been told me of the Venetian State would break a Heart of Stone."[14] Forced onto the market, the palazzo was sold and subdivided, until, a piece at a time, it was reassembled to become the property of the city of Venice. (Today it is the city-owned Benedetto Marcello Conservatory of Music.)

In this way, fairly little of the Pisani family's centuries of wealth and power remained by the time the younger brother, our Almorò's father, died in Padua in 1836. His son—that Count Almorò Pisani III whom Evelina would marry—inherited a relative pittance. It was a true coming down in the world.

But it was not all bad: to Almorò went the aristocratic title and some vestiges of the grand old ways. Its owners—our Almorò's father and uncle—may have been turned out, but in 1847, Almorò Junior, Evelina's future husband, was smart enough to purchase his own apartment on the Grand Canal. It was on the mezzanine floor of Palazzo Barbaro, one of the most prestigious of all Venetian palazzi, and itself a victim of hard times.

Most importantly for the future of both Evelina and her betrothed, Almorò managed to keep the huge estate at Vescovana near Padua. This was especially important, for, unlike the villa at Strà, its farm crops earned its keep, and Almorò's.

The family's notable collection of ancient medals and coins was much diminished, but Evelina's new fiancé, the Count, still owned vestiges of it, and took signal pleasure in trading and discussing rare coins with like-minded collectors. In his selling and collecting, Almorò was perhaps attempting to rebuild the famous family collection. His interest in his own numismatics collection is revealed in his letters. In one, Almorò confided to Vincenzo Lazzari, the director of the Correr Civil Museum in Venice, "Please forgive my candor, which is due to the passion I have for my collection." Almorò also advised Lazzari that he had sent the museum a gold coin from ancient Rome, "the only one I have."

Coin collecting was a two-way street: in a letter of February 4, 1861, Almorò offered thanks for having received a certain gold coin from Venice, "which was lacking." Further demonstrating the extent of that passion, on January 14, 1862, when he and Evelina had been married for almost seven years, Almorò wrote museum director Lazzari that he was returning a dozen 20-franc gold coins showing the profile of the Doge Marino Faliero (1285-1355).

In July of 1861, he and Evelina traveled to Bath in England. From there he wrote: "I have learned that, through my means, the Counts Ci [?] and Grimani have sold the collection of Venetian coins; this collection included some of the gold coins now lacking from my collection, that is, the Marcello coin [his underscoring], plus a few others which should not have been removed so do get them [back] to me at the price you consider most convenient."

Did the passion for coins have something to do with their meeting and marrying? It is just possible that, from beyond the grave, Evelina's grandfather, the late numismatist cum archaeologist James van Millingen, had had a role in bringing the couple together. While living primarily in Florence, Evelina's grandfather, James, who at the time of her engagement had been dead seven years, had traveled widely and belonged to professional antiquarian associations all over Europe. Fascinated by numismatics as a boy, for decades James had been both scholar and dealer; he was still selling rare coins to the British Museum in 1839 and 1840, and had published at least five important works on ancient coins. His last, the first ever written on the historic coins and medals from the country he knew best, Italy, was called *Considerations on the Numismatics of Ancient Italy*.

Despite being a doctor in Constantinople, Julius followed in the footsteps of his father James to a remarkable extent. Like his father, Julius became an amateur archaeologist skilled enough to conduct excavations and to lecture in Greek in Pera on archaeology. Julius and his younger and more inept younger brother Augustus in Rome had inherited what was left of their father's fine personal collection, along with the names of those collectors with whom James had dealt. As an enthusiastic young collector, Almorò may have entered into contact with James and subsequently with Julius. If so, it would have been through her father's intervention that Evelina was introduced to her coin-collecting future husband—which would explain why her aunt claimed it was she who had made the match.

Almorò was homely but titled, and, at least by Millingen family standards, apparently wealthy. In his own box at the Fenice Opera Theater, the 37-year-old bachelor would have seen the beautiful, 21-year-old Evelina in her full exotic dress.

Somehow or other the two met. They conquered each other. For both, their wedding the following summer would be their first and only marriage.

But before the wedding came recriminations. The fact is that, after that night at the opera, Evelina did not return home, but lingered in Venice for months—far longer than her father had anticipated. Most seriously, Evelina did not bother to inform Julius that she was engaged to be married. Eventually Evelina's chaperone Mme. Steindl, the friend of the Sturmers, wrote the news to her husband, who was still working at the Austrian embassy in Pera, that Evelina was betrothed. As a result, one day M. Steindl knocked on the door of Julius's home to deliver the news to her father and Adele.

Julius was outraged at this circumvention of his parental rights. He immediately sat down to pen a letter of reproach to Evelina, dated Oct. 20, 1852 (the original is in the archives of the van Millingen-Backhouse family). "I was truly happy to receive news of you, indirectly," he wrote acidly. The junior diplomat Steindl had given Evelina's father this news "with a most mortified look." Presumably forgetting that he had rarely written his daughter in Rome, Julius complained that in all those months she was in Venice, he had received "only one letter from you, my very dear Evelina."

His wife Adele also disapproved of his daughter's behavior, Julius added, which revealed, or so he said quoting Adele, Evelina's unfortunate "Latin and Greek" background—that is, her French and Greek genetic-cultural heritage from Marionca's side of the family. In the end of this long missive, Julius wishes his daughter, despite misgivings over her future husband's Catholic religion, to seek help from Providence in deciding "what in the end will be best for your present, and above all your future, happiness, at the end of this enterprising episode of your existence."

With this letter, he enclosed two from her aunt Cornelia. Obviously already informed that Evelina had remained far longer in Venice than originally planned, Cornelia dismissed Evelina's time in Venice as a mere "escapade"— an escapade until the two were married, when she claimed it was her own doing.

It was not yet over. That spring found Evelina still in Venice, together with her somewhat reluctant chaperone and, naturally, the Sturmers. On March 10, 1853, Ros Steindl wrote Julius "and Madame Millingen" that she was sorry not to have written them personally before this, but that her right hand had developed very painful arthritis, and she could not write at all. (This ignores that it was her letter to her husband which let the engagement cat out of the bag). "I understand it must be painful for you to be without her," wrote Ros, "and I am waiting with impatience to see my husband again, I've truly suffered from this long separation. He has written to me with pleasure of your friendship."

Eventually, of course, Julius forgave his daughter. The wedding, consequence of Evelina's "escapade," did not happen instantly, however. Before the two could marry, Julius, having accepted the marriage on principle, was obliged to come up with a dowry. He eventually, did, albeit considerably later. A year passed before the bans were published in Venice on three days in mid-June of 1853.

The wedding took place on July 7 in a church not far from the Piazza San Marco, Santa Maria del Giglio, or Saint Mary of the Lily, a reference to the traditional flower held by the angel of the Annunciation. It was a church with a family connection, for Almorò—who now owned a flat within the Palazzo Barbaro—was a distant relation by marriage of the Barbaro family.

A reconciled father, Julius van Millingen, traveled from Constantinople to give away the bride; surely Evelina's Aunt Cornelia also came from Rome, given that the wedding took place in a Catholic church.

If so, the pious Cornelia may have been scandalized at her first glimpse of this church of Santa Maria del Giglio, whose richly ornamented facade successfully avoids any reference to Christianity or any other religion. The church originally dates from the tenth century and was (and is) at the same time one of the city's most beautiful and most peculiar. In the mid-seventeenth century, Venetian Admiral Antonio Barbaro had fought the Turks of Constantinople so successfully that in the course of a single battle, he destroyed 84 Ottoman ships. When the admiral died in 1689, he left a bequest of 30,000 ducats to rebuild the church in celebration of himself along with detailed written instructions for its reconstruction.

The result is an ornate marble baroque facade celebrating the admiral's achievements. A statue of the admiral himself stands in a central niche, while guarding the church corners are statues of his four brothers (Carolus, Francesco, Giovanni Maria, and Marinus). Also on the façade are stone panels bearing still fascinating relief maps of the victorious battles where the admiral had triumphantly served the Venetian Republic: Padua, Corfu, Split (Spalato to the Italians), Candia (Heraklion), and Zadar, in Croatia.

Among the most interesting of these panels is a map of Rome, which could not have escaped Evelina's eye, and which may even have brought her a twinge of nostalgia. It was there because, before becoming admiral, Antonio had been the ambassador of Venice to the pope. The map in stone clearly shows the fortressed walls of Rome which enclose the rippling Tiber River, the Colosseum, and, next to Castel St. Angelo, a carefully executed St. Peter's Basilica facing onto Bernini's colonnades. One corner is devoted to a small relief of Romulus and Remus being suckled by the she-wolf. And, from a few steps away at Evelina's girlhood home in Palazzo Odescalchi, are stone reliefs of Trajan's Column and the Capitoline Hill.

In case anyone missed the point, topping all this on the facade like a cherry on a cake is, instead of a saint or cross, the Barbaro family's (only slightly) cleaned-up family coat of arms, again in marble.

This boastful celebration of the Barbaro family struck that frequent English visitor to Venice, art critic and historian John Ruskin (1819-1900), as so secular that he called it "insolent atheism."

Inside the church, its decorations are more appropriately pious, with two works by Jacopo Tintoretto and a stunning "Madonna with Child and Saint John," the sole painting in Venice by Peter Paul Reubens, who had come there as a youth to study the works by Titian, Veronese, and Tintoretto.

For her wedding, Evelina did not dress overtly *à la Turque*, yet wore a vaguely Oriental-touched creamy silk gown with bouffant sleeves and a demure necklace of stunningly large pearls. The embroidery on the dress looks distinctly Turkish, and, to hold her long veil, she wore an embroidered, pearl-festooned cap that looked as if made by a dressmaker in Pera (as it surely was). In her wedding photograph, she looks beautiful and slender, but also still reveals the shyness which her brother Frederick has mentioned. Their witnesses, according to the marriage register, were the groom's brother Francesco Pisani and the Marchese Stefano Guiccioli.

Of course, Evelina was to have a dowry, which Julius, however, paid only after the wedding, not before. This system of payment had become a common custom in Victorian England. Commerce ruled in that era; whether a marriage was for love (as in the case of Evelina and Almorò), or arranged, money mattered, and never more than among the old and ever more impoverished Venetian nobility. Her new husband acknowledged receipt of the dowry payment, in a letter handwritten in French, dated July 29, 1853. Under the address at the top of the page, "Reigne de Lombardie e Venetie," Almorò writes that he has received the "effective sum of twenty thousand French francs, by way of a dowry contribution [as] established by Docteur G. Millingen for his daughter Madame Evelyn Millingen, now Comtesse Pisani."

Now the deed was truly done. As a bizarre footnote, parish records of Santa Maria del Giglio reveal that Evelina had been presented for marriage as a "Catholic spinster" 22 years of age, with the name of Miss Teresa Evellin Berengaria Millingen, daughter of Dr. Julius and "the late" Mme. Dejean.

Evelina's mother, of course, was very much alive in Turkey and as lively as ever; despite Frederick's eagerness to communicate and his mischievous nature, it is unlikely but not impossible that Evelina actually believed her mother was dead. Certainly Julius knew she was alive, but for him it must have appeared a diplomatic necessity to declare in Venice that his scandalous former wife Marionca was dead.

But again—never mind. The new Contessa Evelina, flung from pillar to post, from Constantinople to Rome and back to Constantinople, now had a home—her own home, and for the first time. Her third life was beginning.

Life on the Lagoon

Already the money-consuming Pisani villa at Strà had been sold to Napoleon. Then the great Palazzo Pisani, itself facing onto the Piazza Santo Stefano, was sold off piecemeal, to become eventually, as it is today, a music academy owned by the City of Venice. So that it too could be sold, the palazzetto with its gondola entrance had again been splintered away from the main palazzo; only the stone Pisani crest on the Grand Canal façade remained to remind passersby of the former grandeur of the Pisani di Santo Stefano.

But despite the loss of the family properties in Venice, Almorò still had other arrows to his bow. After the death of his father in October of 1847, he had inherited the large but run-down plantation at Vescovana in the Veneto. With what income the farm earned, and with the vestiges of profit from the sale of the villa at Strà to Napoleon, Almorò was able to acquire an elegant mezzanine floor apartment of the Palazzo Barbaro, which gives onto the Grand Canal.

This, which Almorò had purchased four years before Evelina's arrival in Venice, is where the couple lived after their marriage in 1853.

In what was her own first home, Evelina did what every other bride of her time did: she began to cut, sew, and embroider a tiny layette for the baby the couple longed to have, to carry on the Pisani name. While awaiting the baby's arrival, Evelina was once again obliged to adjust to the dimensions of what was, for her, an entirely new universe. This was the third radical change in her short life. It was one thing to pass a few months as a visitor to Venice, quite another to live there permanently.

The differences between the lagoon city and her homes in Rome and Constantinople were physical, beginning with the challenge of having to move about primarily on waterways. But those differences were also cultural, political, historical, economical, social, and, not least, linguistic: the language spoken by the Venetians was often virtually incomprehensible to others on the Italian peninsula, who spoke their own dialects (there were as yet no Italians). Her sole link to her past in Constantinople were her dear friends, the Sturmers; otherwise she had to create a new circle of affections and friendships.

Even religion was different. Venetian Catholicism was a far cry from the version Evelina had learned in the papal Rome of convent and her grandmother's highly-placed friends in the Vatican, among them cardinals. Venetian Catholicism was *sui generis*, its centuries of faith colored by repeated open defiance of Rome and of its pontiff rulers. In 1309, Pope Clement V had gone so far as to excommunicate the entire city—and then to launch against Venice nothing less than a crusade.

This did not hinder Venice from continuing to defy such papal orders as, for instance, the Venetians' claim to the right to judge priests in their own, secular tribunals. For their insolence, Venice was excommunicated for the second time in April of 1606, this time by Pope Paul V.

Evelina could not have entirely ignored all this. As she walked through the Campo Santa Fosca in the Cannaregio quarter of Venice, she would have seen high on a pedestal the brooding statue of Father Paolo Sarpi (1552-1623). On that very spot, the priest, a scientist friend of Galileo Galilei, and at the same time a theologian who had dealings in Rome with several popes, but who insisted upon separation of church and state, had been stabbed fifteen times in 1607. The attempted assassination by Vatican hired killers was to punish him for having challenged a papal brief that had ordered unconditional Venetian obedience to Rome. After being stabbed, Sarpi was left for dead, and the pope praised his assailants—or did until learning that Sarpi had survived. His killers' manqués were so disgraced that Rome denied them asylum, and they found refuge only in Naples.

Then there was the plague of 1630, which killed 80,000 Venetians, on a single day. On November 9, almost 600 died. What was to be done with the bodies? *"Chi ga' morti in casa li buta zoso in barca"*—"Whoever's dead in the house, throw them into a boat," advised a doctor, Alvise Zen, who kept a diary of the plague. Today's archaeologists have excavated the island of the Lazzaretto Nuovo, where up to 10,000 plague victims at a time were first quarantined, then buried.

This was Venice. Evelina could have known very little at the outset about these vicissitudes, but they would profoundly affect her life and her husband's in every way imaginable and unimaginable.

The most grievous problems that would come to haunt both Evelina and Almorò began with politics. Following Napoleon's defeat in 1815, Metternich wrested control over Lombardy, Tuscany, the duchies of Modena and Parma, and the Veneto. All these became Habsburg provinces ruled from Vienna. The two Northeastern regions, Lombardy and the Veneto, were the most densely populated, and had rich agricultural production. Lombardy was, in addition, a crossroads on the Italian peninsula and had as a result developed considerable commercial savvy; its capital, Milan, was already the wealthiest commercial city in Italy.

For the Venetians, "structural poverty," as social historians of post-Napoleonic Venice call it, affected every element of their lives. The Veneto was already lagging behind the rest of Northern Italy when excessively harsh Austrian taxation aggravated their plight. By 1848, the Kingdom of Lombardy-Venetia was home to one-sixth of all the subjects under Habsburg rule, but, most unfairly, Venetian citizens provided the monarchy in Vienna with almost one-third of their tax revenues. If Lombardy could possibly afford this, the Veneto could not.

For Venice, the sea had been the source of its wealth for nine centuries. But by the mid-nineteenth century, when the industrial revolution was in full sway on mainland Northern Italy, only small craft could enter the city's two main ports, the Lido and Treport. The difficulties of obtaining such industrial essentials as fresh water and coal, and of transporting these by gondola to Venice, and then of returning the finished goods to the mainland for sale, boosted beyond measure the cost of manufacturing goods of any type.

Furthermore, even when the finished goods reached the mainland by boat, the roads toward markets were poor. It was a further crushing blow that the inland Lombards, with their bustling new factories, favored the port at Genoa even as the Austrians promoted the port at Trieste at Venetian expense. Venice was left "on the periphery," in the words of Venetian historian Adolfo Bernardello.

Some Venetians tried to compete. In 1840, a Venetian businessman imported machinery from England so as to manufacture carpets and bolts of felt. But there was insufficient local consumption, and within three years, two-thirds of his factory work force of 300 were fired and 34,000 meters of unsold fabric were left to rot.[2]

Construction of a new railway bridge in 1846 was supposed to boost Venetian fortunes by creating the first ever waterless link between the lagoon city and the cities on the mainland. The goal of this railway link was to expedite postal communications as well as to ship goods from Venice's few new factories to Verona, where the railway connected with Lombardy and the Veneto, and through the Brenner Pass to Northern Europe.

But not even this sufficed to save Venice, as is shown by a 25% decline in its population in a dozen years (that is, from perhaps 126,000 in 1836 to under 106,000 in 1848).[3] A decade later the losses had not been recouped. Furthermore, Venetian trade, ship building, and its other local industries tended to have passed into the hands of outsiders, with many among the Venetians cut out of what business there was. Of a dozen insurance agencies in Venice at mid-century, all had headquarters elsewhere in the Habsburg Empire—one in Milan, one in Vienna, and seven in Trieste, the Austrian port of preference.

Metternich had famously declared that Italy was nothing more than a "geographical expression" lacking political cohesion or even significance.

➤ Countess Evelina.

Ripped from its piers by storms in 1882, the Ponte Nuovo at Verona. The high waters left 200,000 homeless and endangered Vescovana

◄ Young Julius,
born in Paris, would
become Evelina's father.
Painting on ivory.

◄ After the death of Lord
Byron, Dr. Julius van
Millingen remained in
the service of the Sultan
in Constantinople.

▲ Rome's fifteenth century Palazzo Odescalchi by Piranesi (left), where Evelina lived with her grandmother, across the street from the Basilica of the Holy Apostles.

➤ James van Millingen (1774–1775), Evelina's Dutch–English grandfather, was an antiquarian and archaeologist.

◄ Elizabeth van Millingen, Evelina's grandmother, was separated from husband James, partly over religious differences.

▼ Julius van Millingen and children land in Constantinople harbor in 1837 after four months at sea from Italy.

◄ Dr. Julius van Millingen was in the employ of five sultans.

➤ From Rome, Julius's sister Cornelia came to Constantinople to help tend to the children.

◄ Evelina at age 20 in Constantinople.

➤ Visiting Venice, Evelina was the guest of Viennese diplomat Bartholomaus von Sturmer and his wife Ermance.

▲ Newly rebuilt after a fire, at
La Fenice opera house (print
from 1837) aEvelina in her exotic
attire stunned the Venetians.

➤ Wedding portrait,
Evelina, who wed Almorò
Pisani in 1853 in Venice.

◄ The couple were married in Santa Maria del Giglio, a church built by the venerable Barbaro family, relatives of Almorò.

▼ Palazzo Pisani, ancestral home of the descendants of the 114th Doge of Venice Alvise Pisani (1664–1741)

➤ Count Almorò Pisani III, Evelina's husband, descendant of the doge Alvise Pisani.

▼ Railroad bridge, Venice, built in 1846. Via this train the Pisani traveled to Padua.

▲ Historic Palazzo Barbaro on the Grand Canal, a center of international high society, where Evelina and Almorò occupied a huge mezzanine flat.

◄ Evelina with a pet monkey.

◄ Frederick van Milligen,
her difficult brother,
converted to Islam
and assumed the name
"Osman Seify Bey".

➤ Portrait of Evelina.

Evelina's husband Count Almorò died at age 65 while the couple were visiting the Pisani estate at Vescovana.

➤ Poet John Addington Symonds (1840-1893), close friend of Evelina and pioneer for gay relations, "that unmentionable custom".

❥ American-born Daniel Sargent Curtis (1825-1908) and his wife Ariana (*right*) purchased all but Evelina's portion of Palazzo Barbaro, Henry James' setting for *The Wings of the Dove* and the model for Isabella Stewart Gardner's Boston museum.

For her garden Evelina was inspired by Hortus Floridus by the brilliant Dutch horticulturist Crispijn van de Passe (1589–1670).

Exterior, Villa Pisani at Vescovado near Padua. The villa was occupied by German military in the Second World War.

Interior of the restored villa, now known as Villa Pisani Bolognesi Scalabrin.

In Villa Pisani the widowed Evelina (left) was visited by the Empress of Germany, daughter of Queen Victoria.

Evelina's half-brother Professor Alexander van
Millingen (1840–1915) was a distinguished author
and scholar of Byzantine architecture.

Garden Evelina created at Vescovana lives on in lectures, concerts, courses in cuisine
and flower arranging, and in an annual autumn garden show, "Giardinity."

Challenging this view in the late 1840s were the winds of pan-Italian nationalism sweeping the entire peninsula. The wave of nationalism throughout the Italian peninsula, from Piedmont to Palermo—that same nationalism that would have papal Rome proclaimed a republic in 1848, incidentally freeing Evelina and her brothers from the clutches of the papal state—brought new problems. In Milan, the high taxes imposed by the Habsburg regime precipitated the so-called "Tobacco Riots," in which some 10,000 took part in demonstrations.

The hero challenging the Habsburgs in the Veneto had been Daniel Manin, as we have seen in Chapter 5. Following his defeat, the Habsburgs were again in control of Venice, bringing with them fundamental economic problems that continued to punish the lagoon city. "The whole [Venetian nineteenth] century was characterized by alternating inflationist and deflationist cycles or, vice versa, by a protracted, marked deflation," writes historian Bernardello.[4]

It was not only Almorò's branch of the Pisani to suffer. Veronese's "The Family of Darius at the feet of Alexander" had been painted around 1565 for Villa Pisani at Este, near Padua. Queen Christina of Sweden had tried to purchase the painting in the 1660s, but her agent's offer had been rejected as insufficient. Visiting Venice a century later, Goethe too had been captivated by the painting, which he saw while staying at the Villa Pisani. Later, John Ruskin would describe it as the world's "most precious Paul Veronese", the finest painting in the whole Veneto. In 1857, it was sold by the last male descendant of the Pisani Moretta, Count Vettore Pisani. (It is now in London's National Gallery.)

Once rich and powerful Venetian families suffered from the decades of Venetian structural poverty. As a multitude of important palazzi went on the block, real estate values collapsed. The wealthy Lordan family lost their Ca' Loredan on the Grand Canal, a magnificent, five-story palazzo with 70 rooms. In 1857, Augusto Barbesi purchased it for 270,000 lire, intending to convert it into a hotel. But even this businessman could not fight the era's decline of Venice. Within a decade, Ca' Loredan had to be sold at auction for only 93,708 lire, or one-third of its original price. (Today it is a bed and breakfast.)

Evelina and Almorò were more fortunate, for they still owned a genuine cornucopia—the vast farming estate with its impressive, sprawling mansion at Vescovana. The village and the estate lay between the towns of Padua and Rovigo, on a triangle of flatland between the Adige and the Gorzone Rivers (the latter is called a river but in fact is a broad canal built in the seventeenth century). Both flow into the Adriatic Sea south of Venice at Chioggia.

The plantation at Vescovana was what had remained after the more impressive, but also more costly, Villa Pisani at Strà had been sold to

Napoleon. Simple economics explained the choice of which was to be sold: maintenance at Strà was costly, and the sale was profitable, whereas the more modest and shabby Vescovana property earned its keep, and theirs, through the sale of its grain and corn (maize).

During Evelina's early years in Venice, the estate was merely a somewhat rundown farm, and the villa still the family's "Sunday house," as it had been called in documents from centuries before their time. Making their home in the apartment on the Grand Canal in Venice most of the year, they spent summers at Vescovana even though when they were first married, the estate was in "poor condition," as Almorò's farm manager, the *gastaldo*, acknowledged in one of his regular reports giving detailed accounts of agricultural production, rentals to tenants, and the sales of animals.

The *gastaldo* held a unique position in the lives of the Pisani, for he was their overseer cum sheriff, with the authority for local policing. The *gastaldo* was even expected to keep an eye on the workers' social life; his contract with Almorò specified that he was to keep farm workers from hanging out in the local wine shops. Almorò must have personally dictated the clause in the contract which literally forbade the farmers to gossip about his business affairs. In the wording of his contract with the *gastaldo*, "The Count proprietor would take it badly should his employees frequent the cafes and the wine shops, and form bonds of friendship with the village folks, if for no other reason than because his employees would not otherwise be able to keep themselves free and independent of any personal considerations concerning the interests of the Count proprietor."[5]

The Vescovana estate lay within a larger territory which had once belonged to the House of Este at Ferrara. Over the centuries, warring French and Spanish armies had crisscrossed it periodically, slaughtering inhabitants and leaving the land and its little towns like Vescovana in ruins.

In the fifteenth century, the Vescovana plantation had become the property of two Este brothers in the employ of Venice as *condottieri*, or professional warlords. After both were killed in battle, the farm was bought by the Venetian Pisani in 1478. Tradition has it that the first house built there was destroyed three times and each time rebuilt.

Local land ownership records called "*condizioni di decima*" (ten percent taxation requirements) indicate that a half century later, Cardinal Francesco Pisani, bishop of Padua from 1524 to 1567, had built the monumental Villa Pisani seen today—hence the town name, Vescovana (bishop is *vescovo* in Italian).

Rising in the misty flatlands of the Po Valley a short distance from the town, it was fairly grand by 1661, and at that time described as the "Sunday house" (*casa dominicale*) or vacation home for the personal use of the Pisani—"a single corpus with palazzo, archway, orchard, vegetable garden, courtyards, stables, haystacks, market place and workers' cottages."[6] Three stories tall, with two wings jutting out from the main portion of the house so that it was extraordinarily elongated, it was approached even then by a handsome avenue of trees.

After a new "time of peace and prosperity" began, a public outdoor farm market was opened in the abutting village of Vescovana. In Almorò's day, the estate farmers still sold their produce in that village market square once a week, and profits from rental of the space went into his pocket. An official document dated January 8, 1855, when Evelina and Almorò had been married two years, shows that the Pisani themselves had been owners of that piazza space "from time immemorial" and were hence entitled to exact rent from each farmer setting up a stand. This was useful: on market day, the little piazza at Vescovana sported 42 market stalls, according to recent archival research by Maria Elisabetta Piccolo.[7]

For Evelina and her husband, the house and plantation did not come without problems. Only a few days after their wedding, Almorò had received a letter from his property manager, the *gastaldo*, bemoaning the fact that a disastrous flood had occurred. The letter, written just one day before the wedding, was a long litany of complaints. The manager wrote on July 6, 1853:

Although the waters have receded, they have left sad tracts of uncultivated land. The sowing had been poor because the earth was soggy from too much rainfall, and now the flood has swept away the newly planted seeds, so we shall have a poor wheat crop. Expect a dreadful harvest, with little hay, and the grapevines ruined by mold.

Evelina was having none of this hand-wringing. She was barely 22 when she had made her first of many summer visits to the Pisani's huge but shabby Renaissance-era "Sunday house." Those visits had been galvanizing: as well as Almorò's, this was now her home, her land, her flood, her crops, her garden. When the couple had been married just a few months, Evelina began to prod Almorò into making radical improvements, particularly of the garden immediately behind the house.

The following spring, Almorò agreed to hire a garden architect from Padua named Girolama Scanferla, who was to help them plan improvements to the garden. To meet Scanferla, in March of 1854, Evelina and Almorò traveled by train from Venice, crossing the lagoon via the eight-year-old railroad bridge onto the mainland, and from there on to Padua, a journey of almost 27 miles.

Their meeting with the architect took place at the already famous Cafe Pedrocchi, still popular with tourists visiting Padua today. The two-story cafe was, and is, remarkable for its great neo-Classical colonnade, designed in 1831 by Giuseppe Jappelli, a noted Venetian architect, who added a neo-Gothic wing in 1839. Three years later, he topped this enlarged structure with a second story, composed of a series of halls again reflecting the neo-Classical taste of the era. One frescoed room evoked ancient Greece and another, Herculaneum, whose ruins had been known for over a century; the decors of still other halls were inspired by the Renaissance and Baroque eras.

What might have seemed to Evelina like post cards from her childhood was a round room, decorated in 1841 by Ippolito Caffi of Belluno; it featured exquisite wall paintings showing familiar Roman sights: Castel Sant'Angelo overlooking the Tiber River, an ancient Roman temple, and, rising from Trajan's Forum, the Emperor's Column, still standing just one block from where Evelina had lived with her grandmother in Piazza Santi Apostoli.

The Cafe Pedrocchi was already celebrated for its architecture and these paintings, and because its doorway beneath the Doric-style columned entrance was kept open 24 hours a day. In his *The Charterhouse of Parma,* the French author Stendhal (the pen name of Marie-Henri Beyle) had lauded the chilled pudding dessert *zabaglione* served in the café, which he had called the best in Italy, "almost" as fine as any in Paris (*"presque égal"*). Besides its literary fame, the cafe was also renowned because, during the nationalist rebellion only seven years before Evelina's and Almorò's visit there, Habsburg soldiers had fired upon a group of rebellious students. One of their bullets had left a hole in one wall. (It is still there.)

For the previous month, architect Scanferla (perhaps a descendant of the eighteenth century Paduan artist of that name) had been elaborating a project to redesign the garden. When he and the Pisani were settled onto the leather banquettes by one of the round tables, architect Scanferla spread out the plans he had drawn up.

Evelina, by then 23 years old, was not unaccustomed to luxurious surroundings: she could call home two fine Italian buildings, Palazzo Odescalchi in Rome and the palace in Venice, but until now she had never owned a garden, nor even lived near one, save for the somewhat ramshackle one by the wooden house in Pera, for which she had no responsibility nor rights. Now she had both, plus boundless enthusiasm. Ignoring the plans for the garden as being hatched by her husband and the architect, Evelina seized paper and pencil and gleefully but methodically began sketching her own plan for a garden. The garden was to be hers—her project, her design, and hers alone.

The men agreed, however reluctantly, and Evelina began putting her plans into action the following spring. They began on March 2, 1855, when Almorò sent their *gastaldo* a note asking that a certain number of trees be planted near the ice house (that ice house stocked with ice from the nearby Santa Caterina Canal when it froze over). "Enclosed is a note from Evelina about planting seeds for flowers," he added. Later that month he wrote, "I approve of the repairs being done to save the hedges. Maybe all this rainfall will have been good for the plants and hedges in the garden." Two years later, more flowers were planted, again in March, and a little statue of a Madonna was placed at the bottom of the new garden.

A vine with chandelier-like bundles of tiny lavender-hued flowers had been planted over the vaults by the main back entrance to the house. "And how is the climbing wisteria doing?" Almorò queried of the *gastaldo*.

By then Evelina and Almorò were working with Antonio Gradenigo, an artist-decorator born in Padua, and friend and collaborator of none other than the famous architect of the Café Pedrocchi, Giuseppe Jappelli. Gradenigo had worked with Jappelli to create all the elegant interior decorations within the neo-Gothic addition to the cafe. In 1838, together Gradenigo and Jappelli had worked for two years in Rome rebuilding the Casina della Civetta of the Villa Torlonia, in which Prince Torlonia was then living. (Until his arrest in 1943, Mussolini and his family would live in the adjacent great house—the *Casina Nobile*—while the current Torlonia prince remained in the smaller Casina della Civetta—the Owl House.)

Returning to Padua, Gradenigo began to assume some of the functions of an architect, designing, among other projects, monumental cemetery tombs, the high altar for a church in Trento, and the facade for another church at Archella.

His next project for the Pisani plantation began in March of 1857: to build a coffee house (unfortunately now lost). What has remained is a stretch of garden overlooking a canal and a large field planted with oaks, plane trees, and willows. In the center, a fountain was placed, showing the date of its installation, 1869, plus the Pisani coat of arms, and the name "Ermolaus III Comes Pisani," in honor of a famed, early eighteenth century Pisani family numismatist.

In April of 1858, Gradenigo began an important new project: construction of a chapel on the Pisani estate—that chapel in which both Evelina and Almorò would one day be buried.

This, then, was not only the background to Evelina's life in Venice, but also her serious introduction into the arts and architecture.

In 1854, the year after they were married, the couple traveled to Constantinople, where Almorò met Julius's entire brood and his third wife. Of Julius's multitude of children, the most interesting they met during that visit in 1854 was Evelina's half-brother, Alexander (1840-1915). Nine years younger than Evelina, he was the son of Julius's late second wife, Saphiriza, and would soon be sent to England to be educated. Later Alexander would earn a master's degree from his father's university, Edinburgh, and achieve lasting fame for his career as a historian. His book, *Byzantine Constantinople, The Walls of the City*, translated and first published in England in 1899, is recognized as a classic in its field, and was reprinted in 2010 by the Cambridge University Press.

Her education was broadened by their visit to Bath, where they "took the waters" in 1862. Not long after that trip to Bath, Evelina's beloved friend and mentor Ermance Sturmer died in her palazzo in Venice on June 27, 1863, and was buried on the cemetery isle of San Michele. The cemetery island in a lagoon close to Venice proper had been reshaped to form a square surrounded by walls, and with a small harbor inlet for the boats of the funeral mourners. Cypress trees forming avenues crisscross the monumental grave markers.

Only ten days later, Ermance's husband, Barthelemi Sturmer, followed his wife to the grave, and Evelina attended a second, devastating funeral on the same island.

The Sturmers' stone tombstone still stands against a wall of the cemetery. Into it are incised words that say (my translation):

This tomb was not yet sealed when the cinders gathered of Ermance Caterina C. de Sturmer born Baron.ssa Boutet—Woman of fine sentiments and signal piety, born XXV feb 1798, died XXVII giugno 1863—[were] united X days later by her beloved consort Bartolomeo Count de Sturmer born XXVI Xbre 1787 His great mind rose him to the high offices of the state and his goodness of heart blesses his memory.

Confirming that the Sturmers had no children of their own, the tombstone is signed: *I Nipoti*, The Nephews.

Evelina had been their child. Like Ermance, she would have no children of her own. The garden which Evelina began to create in the Café Pedrocchi would be her child, and grow with her.

In Evelina's world, there was no one who could replace the Sturmers. Her relationship with her surrogate mother, Ermance, would remain unique. But to fill the void, at least in part, there were new friends from many different countries. As the attractive and exotic young wife of a Pisani, she became a doyenne of Venetian society, but at the same time she was a cosmopolitan. Far from altogether comfortable in time spent solely with the more or less impoverished, but still snobbish and arrogant, Venetian aristocrats, she began to seek out those whose far more varied backgrounds were akin to her own.

Thanks to the advances in transport, Venetian society had become far more international than ever before, thanks to the lagoon city's exuberant culture and centuries of great artists. However poor the native Venetians, after the fall of Napoleon, Venice remained for the rest of the century an exciting international gathering place which nurtured poets, painters, architects, and musicians from all over Europe and beyond. Most importantly, as the industrial revolution made factories ubiquitous elsewhere, the very elements of Venetian decadence became appealing to those living in more modernized societies.

As a result, among the frequent visitors to Venice after 1858—and these prestigious visitors attracted others of their kind—was Richard Wagner, who lived in a double palazzo at Ca' Giustiniana, in which he wrote Act Two of *Tristan and Isolde*. Wagner was often seen in the eighteenth century Café Florian or in another of the cafes in the Piazza San Marco. He died in Venice in the Ca' Vendramin Calergi at age 69 in 1883, the year after completing *Parsifal*.

Lord Byron had similarly spent, or, as we have seen, misspent years in Venice, where he met and fell in love with Teresa Guiccioli. To his publisher in London, John Murray, Byron had written on November 25, 1816, of visiting a café so wicked that it had turn-table trays in a wall so that the servants could not see the goings-on of lascivious patrons.[8] Byron's attitude toward Venice was ambiguous; his famous poem "Childe Harold's Pilgrimage" begins with these lines:

I stood in Venice, on the Bridge of Sighs,
A palace and a prison on each hand.

Venice was not the only Italian city, of course, to attract the foreign elite, whose presence there would profoundly affect culture worldwide until our own time. Rome was foremost, and in the same period the writers Stendhal and Honoré Balzac frequented the salon of just one of the many Roman aristocrats, Duke Michelangelo Caetani (1802-1882). Others in the Caetani circle were French historian François-René de Chateaubriand; German historians Theodor Mommsen and Ferdinand Gregorovius; novelist Sir Walter Scott; and Lord John Acton from England, who would become a prominent professor of history at Cambridge. From the United States was the poet Henry Wadsworth Longfellow.[9]

However attractive Rome, Venice had its own appeal. None was more influential in attracting cultivated mid-nineteenth century visitors to Venice than England's leading art historian, John Ruskin, whose *The Stones of Venice*, an extremely detailed study of Venetian art and architecture, was published between 1851 and 1853. Ruskin loved Venice all the more because of his hostility to the "ugliness of industrialisation, urbanisation, and poverty of a developing capitalist Europe."[10] This hostility to industrialization would draw other outstanding creative individuals to Venice, and into the circles frequented by Evelina. It would be toward their world that Evelina gravitated following the death of the Austrian Sturmers.

Together with his wife, Ruskin visited Venice for three winters in a row. Each winter produced a new volume in which Ruskin not only meticulously described churches, palazzi, and paintings, but, taking his own daguerreotype photographs and making his own sketches, provided illustrations to accompany his text. His text is also engaging:

And now come with me, for I have kept you too long from your gondola: come with me, on an autumnal morning, to a low wharf or quay at the extremity of a canal, with long steps on each side down to the water, which latter we fancy for an instant has become black with stagnation; another glance undeceives us, —it is covered with the black boats of Venice. We enter one of them, rather to try if they be real boats or not, than with any definite purpose, and glide away; at first feeling as if the water were yielding continually beneath the boat and letting her sink into soft vacancy.[11]

Writing of a single side of one column capital in a Venetian church, he describes a stone carving of the moon, which he reports as particularly picturesque. He writes:

The moon is represented as a woman in a boat, upon the sea ... [who] raises the crescent in her right hand, and with her left draws a crab out of the waves, up the boat's side.
The moon was, I believe, represented in Egyptian sculptures as in a boat; but I rather think the Venetian was not aware of this, and that he meant to express the peculiar sweetness of the moonlight at Venice, as seen across the lagoons.

What could be more evocative? Among those Ruskin most influenced was William Morris, the leader of the Victorian Arts and Crafts Movement, which began in 1880 in Britain. Not least, he influenced Henry James, who would become a center of Venetian international society, and a friend of Evelina.

In the meantime, life for Evelina was rich, and, to others in her circle, enriching. On lazy summer days, the Pisani gondola would waft them off to far islets, where fellow Venetian aristocrats had servants set out chairs and tables outfitted with elaborate finery for a picnic; they dined under a wisteria bower one day in June, at the splendid Villa Vendramin on the Giudecca with, among others, Paul Bourget of the French Academy, inventor (he created a typesetting machine), J. S. Paige of Rochester, New York, and the poets Elizabeth and Robert Barrett Browning. On autumn mornings, the Venetian grandees, including even women, would meet to chat and to sip coffee and smoke cigarettes in the cafes of Piazza San Marco. Evenings brought music: either grand opera at the Fenice or a concert of chamber music by Schubert or

Mozart, under a painting, perhaps by Veronese, in the hall of the *piano nobile* of one of the great palazzi.

Not least there was work on the garden—her garden, her child—at their villa. Save for their lack of a real child, life itself was, for the Count and Countess Pisani, a gondola glide along a sunny lagoon of joy.

But there were grim shadows elsewhere. During those two decades, Evelina's far-away mother Marionca had suffered myriad catastrophic vicissitudes. After being cast away by her husband Julius, Marionca had traveled from Italy to Paris, where she had met the powerful man she would marry, and who was now known as his Highness Kibrizli-Mehmet-Pasha. But in the scandalous wake of the butler's murder, which had taken place on Marionca's watch and in her home, Kibrizli too had repudiated Marionca.

After the murder, Marionca had been put on trial and exiled far from Constantinople. Kibrizli speedily remarried, taking a new Turkish wife named Ferideh. This was not her first marriage, for Ferideh had a teenaged son. The boy lived with the couple, and so did Aisha, the daughter of Marionca and Kibrizli, and hence Evelina's French-Turkish half-sister.

In 1857, four years after Evelina's marriage, Kibrizli and his new wife, Ferideh, forced the unwilling teenaged Aisha to marry Ferideh's son in Constantinople. The plan was evidently to keep all possible money in the family; were Aisha to marry an outsider, Kibrizli would have to provide her with a dowry.

The marriage plunged Aisha into deepest misery, to the point that she began to hope that her mother Marionca was somehow still alive, and not dead, as her father and stepmother had told her. Seeking help, Aisha confided in an older woman servant, who eventually returned to whisper the news that, yes, Marionca was very much alive. Through this woman, Aisha managed to make contact with, and then to meet, her mother, who later wrote, "The account which my daughter then gave me of her own sufferings nearly broke my heart."

Alas, the cunning stepmother Ferideh realized that something was afoot, and began a campaign denigrating Aisha's reputation to her father. The result was that Kibrizli, convinced his child-bride daughter was dishonoring his name, gave the girl a severe beating. That Aisha suffered mattered little to Kibrizli: "I would far rather mourn her death for 40 days than live dishonoured for the rest of my life," he said (so Marionca records).

Fearing worse was to come, Aisha bolted. At four o'clock in the morning she jumped from a two-story roof into the garden, and managed to land unscathed. Albeit pursued by Kibrizli's slaves as she ran away, she eventually managed to reach her mother, Marionca. Kibrizli was a government minister, and the subsequent gossip did his reputation little good. For years, therefore, intending to show that he was in the right, he and his minions continued to seek Aisha.

Nevertheless, the year 1864 found Aisha, her mother, and younger brother, Djehad, who was also Kibrizli's son, living together, apparently contentedly, in a house with a garden in the suburbs of Scutari, on the Asian side of the Bosphorus, where, incidentally, Florence Nightingale had created her hospital. The garden, as Marionca records, had orange trees and offered a view of the Bosphorus. (There was no news of Marionca's son James, who had been sent to Rome after the other two, but, it is assumed, had died in early childhood.)

There Frederick caught up with his mother and his half-siblings. One wonders if he told them much of his recent past, which had been as dramatic as it was eccentric. For a time, he had, in defiance of his father Julius's express wishes, been a British Army Major, and had written a scurrilous pamphlet against his father entitled "Sin and its victim."[12]

From England, Frederick then moved back to Istanbul, where he converted to Islam, renamed himself "Osman Seify Bey" and joined the Turkish army. Given the rank of Major, he took command of 300 Albanians and was sent with them to Kotur to quell a Kurdish rebellion. In apparent sympathy with Kibrizli-Pasha, or perhaps hoping to benefit from identification with him (or, better, to obtain Kibrizli's money), Frederick then began to call himself Kibrisli-zade Osman Seify Bey (the spellings vary). Later, he occasionally claimed that he was actually Kibrizli's son and, in another version, had married into the Kibrizli family.

Family papers also record that, while in Constantinople after the Kurdistan adventure, Frederick had "abducted a lovely Circassian from the household of Princess Adile Sultana, a sister of Sultan Medjid." This lovely Circassian had just delivered Frederick's baby, whom they named Ishmael, but whom the eloping couple abandoned in the harem nursery. The Janissaries, who were the sultan's personal bodyguard troops, raced after Frederick and the woman escaping with him. They caught up with the two, seized her, and returned her to the harem.

From the nursery, the infant was handed over to Julius and Adelaide, who renamed him Orledge and raised him in their ever-crowded household. Orledge Millingen grew up to become a major in the British Army in World War I, then migrated to the U.S. Before he died at Martha's Vineyard in 1950, Orledge told a van Millingen descendant, John Balfour, that when he had been returned to the nursery, he had been branded on his bottom.[13]

This latest misadventure in Turkey obliged Frederick to bolt once more. From Turkey, he went this time to the Balkans, where he changed his name again, becoming somehow Greek and taking the name Vladimir Alexis Andrejevich, prefaced by the military title "Major."

As if all this baggage did not suffice, Frederick brought to his mother and siblings other problems, far worse than being, as his father said woefully, a "beggar." At that point, Frederick, aka Major Vladimir Alexis Andrejevich, was wanted in seven countries by police, whom he skillfully dodged.

The peaceful respite for the four in the house with the garden on the Bosphorus was brief. Almost without funds at that point, they were warned that Kibrizli knew their whereabouts and was preparing to have them all thrown into a prison fortress called Demitoka, "generally known as a sort of hell on earth," in Marionca's words.[14] One reason she gave was his fear that his daughter Aisha would escape to the West, where infidels would see her face.

Terrified, the quartet vowed to leave Turkey as soon as possible, to return to Paris, Marionca's birthplace. Paris had a thriving Ottoman community, for the city held a special place in the Ottoman world. French, taught in Turkish secondary schools, was the key language which allowed the vital communications, including for trade, between the Ottomans and the West. Moreover, France had been an Ottoman ally during the Crimean War of the early 1850s over control of the Black Sea. To defeat the Russians, the Ottoman Empire had allied itself with France, England, and Sardinia (a unified Italy was yet to come).

For Marionca, her children, and Frederick, the problem was that to flee to Paris required passports, which they had absolutely no way of obtaining. However, friends tipped Marionca off that, if they could find a way to travel aboard the same ship as the French ambassador, the passport requirement would be ignored because he represented the French ally, Napoleon III. "The presence on board of the representative of the Emperor of the French was for us a protection," Marionca later wrote, "as the honour of his flag could not permit force to be used on board a vessel where he himself was present."[15]

The four nervously awaited word that the French ambassador was preparing to leave by ship. When it came, they hastily prepared to leave Constantinople forever. So as not to be noticed by Turkish police, all were dressed European style. For the ladies, this meant petticoats and bonnets, which were provided by Marionca's sister, who still lived in Pera.

Quivering with fear, they approached the ship. Miraculously, and by clever manipulations of Marionca's Turkish nephew, all four—Marionca, Aisha, Djehad, and Frederick—were able to steal aboard, unnoticed.

By the autumn of 1866, they had survived the sea voyage, and were in Paris, where they received at least temporary hospitality in a convent.

In Paris, Frederick van Millingen, who was not without talent, wangled his way into a job as a freelance journalist with *Muhbir*, the newspaper published for the large Ottoman Turkish colony established there. Now writing under the pseudonym Osman Bey, in 1870 he would publish the book *Wild Life among the Koords*, during the troubles in Kurdistan. Then came *Les imams et les derviches: pratiques, superstitions et moeurs des Turcs*. Yet another of his books would be *The Conquest of the World by the Jews*, whose racism—perhaps in defiance of his father Julius—belied his own Jewish heritage. Not least, he penned a pamphlet describing Aisha's misfortunes at the hands of Kibrizli, *Les malheurs et la fuite de Aisse' Chanum Effendi, fille de son altesse Kibrizli-Mehmet, Pacha et Grand Vizir, de 1862 a 1869.*

In Paris, there was never enough money, and so, in 1867, Frederick decided to go to Venice "to compel the Countess Pisani to help her mother. I knew well there was no relying on her feelings, but I hoped that as proud a woman as she would yield to considerations of human respect."[16]

Learning somehow of his son Frederick's plans, from Constantinople Dr. Julius van Millingen sent a letter dated May 3, 1867, via Trieste, to his daughter. In his letter her father warned Evelina that her brother Frederick was now in Paris, and might try to be in touch with her. At all costs, Julius wrote, Evelina must beware of Frederick. The problem was that, by the time their father's letter arrived, Frederick, the boy with whom Evelina had shared her childhood years in Palazzo Odescalchi in Rome, had already arrived in Venice, and was staying at the Hotel Luna. From there, he wrote his sister a shattering letter in which he said that their mother, Marionca, half-sister, and half-brother were now in Paris, and so penniless they risked having to be on public charity.

The shock at receiving this news was devastating. Evelina had been told that her mother was dead. Whether or not she had fully believed that story, it had been confirmed on her wedding certificate, making this the version accepted in Venice by her aristocratic peers for the thirteen years of their marriage. At any rate, it was as if her mother were truly dead, for Evelina had not seen Marionca since childhood. It is doubtful that she knew anything of Aisha or Djehad. When Evelina had married into the world of the Pisani, she had left all this behind, shed off like a filthy old cloak.

Later Frederick related that in Venice,

> I went to the auberge La Luna and from there wrote a letter to our mother [Marionca in Paris]. I put her [Evelina] in a position to help our mother with money … The Pisani [Evelina], on receiving this letter, pretended to suffer attacks of hysteria, she created a pathetic scene, and obliged Count Alomore to have recourse to the police.

Almorò in fact did contact the police. But at that point Marionca too had arrived in Venice from Paris, and the police action was delayed. As Frederick later wrote, the police summoned by Count Pisani had intended "to treat me as an adventurer, extorting money under false pretenses," but did nothing save to order Frederick and Marionca to leave Venice within 24 hours.

But that was not the end of the story, for Evelina must have had misgivings. She found herself unable to reject altogether her brother's appeal, nor the chance to see her mother once more, albeit not in plain sight in Venice.

Almost immediately after Frederick and Marionca had left for Paris, Evelina followed them, accompanied by Almorò.

There, for the first time in a quarter century Evelina met the mother she had been told was dead. She met her two previously unknown half-siblings. And she must have had contact with her eccentric brother, Frederick, for the Count and Countess Pisani lingered in Paris many days before returning to Venice.

Somehow Julius was apprised that his daughter and son-in-law had gone to Paris. In a letter dated May 30, 1867, Julius wrote his daughter to express his "chagrin" that she should have gone to Paris to see her mother. But by then she had returned to Venice, and Julius concluded that he was happy that she was once again home among her own "household gods."

> I congratulate you and Count P. on having treated him [Frederick] as he deserves. I know to my own expense how little his promises are worth. Better if others had followed your example, instead of encouraging him by lavishing help on him. People like him will never reform as long as they meet dupes.

Next on her agenda, Julius suggested, Evelina should pay a visit in Rome to see to her "dear" Aunt Cornelia. "Don't forget to tell her I am thinking of her fondly." Thus, Julius expected Evelina to make peace on his behalf with the woman who had helped raise his first-born, but whom he himself had been cast out of the house in Pera because she had allowed a Catholic priest to cross his threshold. But never mind: Frederick, at least, had been put out of their lives—if only for a time.

Other events began to crowd into the lives of the van Millingen family in Constantinople. In 1870, four years after the unfortunate Paris interlude, their roomy house was burned to the ground, one of thousands of wooden dwellings lost in what has gone done in history as the Great Fire of Pera.

This occurred during the same year when Rome had become absorbed into the new Italy, formally recognized in January of 1871, completing unification of the peninsula.

In 1872, Chapman and Hall of London published a two-volume autobiography by Marionca, entitled *Thirty Years in a Harem*, in English. The author was listed as "Melek-Hanum, Wife of H. H. Kibrizli-Mehemet Pasha." As it happened, Marionca was scarcely literate, and the writing was quite possibly the work of Louis-Alexis Chamerovzow (1816-1875), a well-known author and journalist who lived in Paris. Chamerovzow, of Russian descent but born in Brighton, was a noted anti-slavery campaigner, and in 1848 had published a book on the plight of New Zealand Aborigines, followed by a well-received book on John Brown called *Slave Life in Georgia* in 1855.

However, by 1871, slavery had ended in many countries, and anti-slavery campaigns were no longer popular, so Chamerovzow had ever fewer paying jobs.

Female slavery in the Ottoman world, however, had remained a popular theme with artists and writers. In a vibrant and lengthy description of harem life in her book's Chapter 13, either Marionca (who by then had reconverted to Christianity), or, more likely, Chamerovzow, taking dictation from her, wrote that girl slaves "are sold usually at about twelve or thirteen years of age, but there are cases of sales at the early age of six or seven." The book was a success in her time, and is still being read in the West by students of slavery and of the harem. (It was most recently republished in English in 2005 by Elibron Classics, a listing of the Adamant Media Corp. of Berlin).

Did Kibrizli himself and Julius know of this book? Indeed, they both did, for a lengthy contemporary review of *Thirty Years* appeared in the English-language daily *The Levant Herald* of Constantinople on Sept. 16, 1872. One can only imagine Kibrizli's consternation at its publication, for on the cover her name was linked to his as "wife of H.H. Kibrizli-Mehemet-Pasha". Along with excerpts, the unnamed Turkish reviewer opined that,

> As an author, Melek Hanum is sensationalist and self-serving, plotting her story as a melodrama: a feisty but wronged woman who does her best under adverse circumstances. To some extent this was perhaps an accurate reflection of her situation, since her case clearly attracted considerable interest, or at least notoriety ...
>
> It is firstly and above all an autobiography... and yet, as her story does in point of fact comprise thirty years of harem life it cannot by any means be said that the somewhat catch-penny title which she, or probably her publishers, have chosen for it, is a misnomer. To the general reader, indeed, the main attraction of the volume will doubtless consist in the glimpse which it incidentally affords of the ... Harem. The book can make no pretensions to literary merit.

It is "gossipy" and "slipshod," the reviewer concludes, and untrue, for women are far from being the weaker sex in Turkey: "In truth it may be said that the might of female influence in the making and marring of public man, and the conduct of public affairs, is far greater in this country than in chivalrous Christendom."

Sharp words against his mother came, perhaps surprisingly, from her son Frederick. "I set about publishing in Greek my work 'Mother and Country avenged,' but they at once barred my way by publishing 'Thirty Years in the Harem,' a pseudo-autobiography of my mother's, with the funds put up by reptiles." Reptiles: the publishers who preferred his mother's and her probable collaborator's work to his own. (Nevertheless, say family records, Frederick at one point claimed that he himself had written *Thirty Years*.)[17]

In publishing the book to fanfare, Marionca's goal seems to have been to earn money from sales, but also to pressure Kibrizli into coughing up money to keep her quiet.

That certainly did not work. No sooner was it published than Marionca sat down with the same author to write a sequel, which similarly still attracts the attention of Ottoman-era scholars, *Six Years in Europe, Sequel to Thirty Years in Harem*. This time, Chamerovzow's name appears on the cover as editor, Marionca's as author.

Like hers, his books are still selling.

Dazzling Decadence

Everyone who was anyone in Venice, and particularly the foreigners clustering there, knew Evelina's exotic background, and that of her father, Julius van Millingen, as well. Nothing of her background was ever forgotten, not least by Evelina herself. In the course of one swanky Venetian soiree, Evelina recounted that none other than Teresa Gamba Guiccioli had written to "beg" Evelina to ask her father if he recalled the dying Lord Byron in Turkey making any mention of Teresa.

At age 19, Teresa had briefly met the 24-year-old Byron while visiting Venice, shortly after her marriage in Ravenna in 1818 to a man 40 years older than she. Byron had been living that year in the Palazzo Mocenigo on the Grand Canal with—according to Shelley—"fourteen servants, two monkeys, five cats, eight dogs, a hawk, a crow, two parrots, and a fox, and the whole menagerie goes around the house as if they own it." When they met again in April of 1819, their mutual attraction was evident to both. As Teresa wrote later, "His noble and exquisitely beautiful countenance, the tone of his voice, his manners, the thousands of enchantments that surrounded him, rendered him so different, and so superior a being to any I had hitherto seen, that it was impossible he should not have left the most profound impression upon me. From that evening, during the whole of my subsequent stay in Venice, we met every day."

Three or so days after the two met, Byron himself wrote a friend, "I have fallen in love with a Romagnuola countess from Ravenna." Within days the two were engaging in sex, with all the more freedom because Teresa was already pregnant by her husband.[2]

Teresa Guiccioli was at least the third woman with whom Byron had fallen in love during that Venetian year, but their relationship was, as he instantly realized, special. He followed Guiccioli to Ravenna, and later she came to Venice to live with him. For a time, her husband refused to divorce her, but she and Count Guiccioli were eventually separated, and Byron and Teresa lived openly and traveled together until the poet left for Greece in 1823. After his death, she traveled to England to visit his tomb.

One legendary story has it that on his death bed, a delirious Byron murmured, "There are ... things which make the world dear to me." Was this "thing" Guiccioli? She must have believed so, which would explain why she wrote Evelina.

On receiving the letter from the now elderly Guiccioli, Evelina obediently wrote her father to ask. Yes, Julius wrote Evelina, the dying Lord Byron had mentioned the Contessa, his lover of a half century before this. When asked if Guiccioli had a special charm, Byron had replied that: "She was a woman who could not say no"—so recounted a less than chivalrous Julius.[3]

La Guiccioli died in 1873, not long after Evelina wrote an embarrassed reply to her query.

But already Evelina's Venetian life was not all picnics on verdant islands or dinner parties in the palazzi of wealthy fellow foreigners. In those years, death came knocking at her own door, again and again.

In 1875, Evelina learned from her brother Frederick that their troubled and troublesome mother, Marionca, had committed suicide in Paris. Coincidentally, Louis-Alexis Chamerovzow, Marionca's co-author of at least one of her two books, died in London in November that same year.

The suicide of a mother, no matter how terrible a mother, was bad enough. But then, far from Evelina, her father Julius died at age 78 on December 1, 1878, in Constantinople. Among the last medical commissions he had been given involved the suspicious death of the Sultan Abdul Aziz. Just five days after being deposed and locked into a tower on May 30, 1876, Abdul Aziz was found dead, his wrists slashed. Dr. Julius was asked to determine whether the cause was suicide or murder. Julius died before he could provide the information requested. (Recently surfaced memoirs suggest that Abdul Aziz was in fact assassinated.)

Dying, Julius left his eldest daughter no inheritance whatsoever, doubtless on grounds that he had advanced her (for him) considerable dowry money and that her husband was wealthy; he had a wife and a whole flock of other, younger, and less well-to-do children to tend to.

Childless Evelina had already lost her beloved Sturmers. She had lost, and to suicide, the mother who had never truly been a mother. She had lost the father whom she had belatedly reclaimed, and adored. And now, on July 17, 1880, her husband Count Almorò himself died at age 65 while the couple were visiting on the estate—their "Sunday House"—at Vescovana. They had been married 27 years.

As if grief were not enough, the newly widowed Evelina found herself saddled with debts left by Almorò. When she and Almorò were first married, the estate at Vescovana had been sorely neglected, and already encumbered by debts, apparently acquired in order to improve the swampy farmland. Almorò continued draining, having the farmland improved while repaying the existing mortgage debts on the property. During those decades, Evelina had remained at a distance from the farm and its management. As her young friend Margaret Symonds has recorded, Evelina "lived wholly in the villa, or driving her ponies away into the hills during the months which she and her husband spent on their Italian estate. Her care had been for her house and garden."[4]

But now that she had inherited both farm and debts, Evelina herself was obliged to repay the farm creditors. How to do so? She had no money of her own and had never worked. Repayment by making the estate turn a profit was the sole possibility—either that or sell the farm estate at Vescovana, the equivalent of selling her own memories of Almorò and her respect for the Pisani heritage.

To restore the farm in the countryside at Vescovana, so as to make the estate more profitable, could be no easy task. It would mean managing hundreds of workers, and dealing with their families. Managing oxen and horses and barns and fields and the produce grown on tenant farms. Handling accounts books—she who had never yet examined a book of accounts.

Before she could address these problems, with Almorò dead, a first concern was his burial.

In the late 1850s, he and Evelina had asked architect Pietro Selvatico Estense and sculptor Antonio Gradenigo (who had worked as an interior decorator on the Café Pedrocchi in Padua) to build a tiny chapel on the estate at Vescovana. Designed in neo-Gothic Tudor style with three naves, the finished chapel had been consecrated in 1860. Here Evelina buried Almorò.

Evelina also managed to find sufficient funds to commission the carving of an almost life-sized statue of her husband. The sculptor she selected, Valentino Panciera Besarel, was well known; his works are scattered throughout his native Veneto, and in his own day also traveled to Philadelphia, Chicago, Paris, Edinburgh, and Vienna. In the statue he carved of Carrara marble, Almorò wears a sword and the uniform of an honorary Vatican courtier. On his chest is a commemorative medal of the 1848-1849 war of independence against Austria—that Austria which had brought the Sturmers, and Evelina herself, to Venice. In one hand is his beret, which looks like a pizza pie, and in the other, a lion (get it? the lion of Venice?). At his feet is carved the Count's beloved and elegant little dog, a *volpino* or spitz.

The statue arrived by train and then boat to Stanghella, where the farm workers turned out en masse to greet it, but were disappointed at seeing that it was inside a crate. Still, the crate was loaded onto a cart, drawn by elaborately barded horses, and draped in the Pisani colors of silver and blue. Houses along the roadway were decorated in bunting. When the statue was finally delivered to the chapel, it was inaugurated with a mass on May 25, 1882; only four months later, the terrible flood struck September 1882, while

Evelina was still staying at Vescovana. On hand for the inauguration was Signor Antonio Monato, who spoke of the late Count's "nobility of heart" in kindness to the farm workers, "even when fortune had turned against them." (Agostino Nani Mocenigo, last to inherit the villa from the Pisani family, donated what is described as this architectural "jewel" to the Vescovana parish in 1994.)

Lonely, with no family by her side, and in deep mourning, at the same time that Evelina was forced to deal with the finances of Villa Pisani, she faced a formidable second challenge: to rebuild her life, and for the fourth time. In her previous three lives, she had been a schoolgirl in Rome, then a debutante in Constantinople, and lastly a socialite bride in Venice. How was she to do this? It was no secret that her fellow Venetian aristocrats were less than fond of her, and still spoke of her dismissively as "la Turquesina," the little Turkish lady.

But Venice had outgrown the Venetians, and it was unlikely that a still beautiful, multi-lingual widowed *contessa* living in a fine palazzo on the Grand Canal would be ignored by the cultivated, rich, English-speaking foreigners who were converging upon Venice at just that time. Forerunners including John Ruskin had noticed Evelina, and had already praised her beauty.

Henry James, who had been visiting Venice since 1869, could do no less; and in a letter to Sarah Butler Wister dated February 27, 1887, five years after Almorò's death, James mentioned meeting "the most remarkable" Evelina, whose beauty as a young woman "must have been extraordinary and still is very striking."[5] At that time she was 56, but, James added, looked no more than 40.

The 1880s were the culminating years of the second Grand Tour, which was considerably more middle class than the first Grand Tour of the previous century and involved Americans. The coming of these foreigners to Italy had been eased by the mid-nineteenth century advent of the iron-hulled steamship. Prodded by the profits deriving from mass migration to the U.S., the steamship companies had rushed to make technical improvements, with the result that after 1870, crossing the Atlantic from New York to Liverpool required only seven or eight days. The starving Europeans made the voyage westward jammed into steerage, while for the return voyage the wealthy Americans basked in the luxuriously-outfitted first-class cabins of the same ships.

The English too descended upon Italy, and especially Rome. Earlier in the century, English intellectuals had tended to disregard Rome by virtue of its well-known ancient decadence. But by the mid-Victorian era this view had been revised, with ancient Rome seen as a positive achievement, which "stands out in the very centre of human history," in the words of the

Cambridge don Sir John Robert Seeley, author of a book first published in 1883, *The Expansion of England,* based on his courses of lectures.[6]

This left Venice to replace Rome as the essence of decadence, but in this case decadence was elevated into a virtue, at least for some foreigners. Although Henry James wrote that Venice is "awfully sad too in its inexorable decay," many cultivated and well-to-do Americans were charmed by the evidence of the financial disasters which had wracked Venice. These Americans had grown tired of the vulgar hustle-bustle of the manufacturing industries at home—those industries which had enriched the likes of steel magnates Henry Clay Frick and Andrew Carnegie. The American expatriates, now spending long months and often years in Venice, took boundless delight in the world-weariness of the lagoon city's stinking roadways of water, its moldering walls, and its ancient churches with their masterpieces *in situ.*

The crumbling of Venice became their vigorous lifeblood, and Venice, the residence of American expatriates, the "children of a new empire of commerce," and an outpost of Boston, in the words of Henry James' biographer, Leon Edel.[7] Rich—particularly by the standards of the *nouveaux pauvres* locals—these adoptive Venetians also indulged their passion for studying and snapping up works of art, many of which later went to enrich America's museums.

Their cultural precursor was John Ruskin, even though, while describing the squalor, he did not particularly romanticize it in his *The Stones of Venice.* Writing in the early 1850s, the art historian deplored the "half stagnant canals ... villas sinking fast into utter ruin, black, and rent, and lonely ... blighted fragments of gnarled hedges and broken stakes for their fencing ... the water, which latter we fancy for an instant has become black with stagnation."[8]

Typical of those romanticizing the decadence of Venice was American expatriate Willian Dean Howells. From 1861 through 1863, Howells lived in Venice, where President Abraham Lincoln had appointed him to serve as American consul. Three years after finishing his tour of duty, Howells published his book *Venetian Life,* in which he celebrated what he called the "interesting squalor" and "pleasant" hopelessness of the filthy Venetian neighborhoods:

> All places had something rare and worthy to be seen: if not loveliness of sculpture or architecture at least interesting squalor and picturesque wretchedness; and I believe I had less delight in proper Objects of Interest than in the dirty neighborhoods that reeked with unwholesome winter damps below, and peered curiously out with frowzy heads and beautiful eyes from the high, heavy-shuttered casements above....
>
> Being newly from a land where everything, morally and materially, was in good repair, I rioted sentimentally on the picturesque ruin, the pleasant discomfort and hopelessness of everything about me here.[9]

Henry James was another bewitched by Venetian decadence, even though Lyndall Gordon, one of James's many biographers, has written that, "The real James remained an American: a visionary moralist [who] did not indulge in the European vogue for decadence."[10] Nevertheless, not without a hint of pleasure, Jamesian prose lingered over the Venice of "the tattered clothes hung to dry in the windows, sun-faded rags that flutter from the polished balustrades ivory-smooth with time." And in 1869, Henry James acknowledged that, "Venice is quite the Venice of one's dreams, but ... It's awfully sad too in its inexorable decay."

> The whole scene profits by the general law that renders decadence and ruin in Venice more brilliant than any prosperity. Decay is in this extraordinary place golden in tint and misery *couleur de rose*.[11]

"Rosy decadence," that is, but also rhapsodic.

His occasionally jaded view of Venice was not the whole story, of course. For, as James himself remarked in his essay on "The Grand Canal," published in *Italian Hours* in 1892, "What is the whole place but a curiosity-shop, and what are you here for yourself but to pick up odds and ends?"

> It is a fact that almost everyone interesting, appealing, melancholy, memorable, odd, seems at one time or another, after many days and much life, to have gravitated to Venice by a happy instinct, settling in and treating it, cherishing it, as a sort of repository of consolations.

These "odds and ends" of the Venetian curiosity-shop were transported by Henry James into the novel *Princess Casamassima* (1886), the novella *The Aspern Papers* (1888), and the conclusion of *The Wings of the Dove*, begun while he was still in England, but completed in Venice.

In the widowed Evelina's day, the first and most important gathering place for these erudite and well-heeled expatriates of England, the United States, and France, too, was the palatial home on the Grand Canal of Sir Austen Henry Layard (1817-1894), an already famous archaeologist. Layard had spent much of his early life in Italy. Moving to Constantinople in 1842, he became a close associate and friend of Sir Stratford Canning, that same ambassador who had worked to free Evelina's father Julius from imprisonment by the pasha.

Encouraged by Canning, Henry Layard developed his passion for and knowledge of archaeology. Leaving Constantinople, Layard explored sites in Assyria, beginning with his excavation of Nimrud on the Tigris, which brought him fame. (Nimrud was tragically destroyed by the Islamic State militants, or ISIS, in March 2015.) Layard then discovered ancient Nineveh, on the eastern bank of the Tigris in today's Iraq, and in 1848 published his two-volume *Nineveh and its Remains: with an Account of a Visit to the Assyrians, and the Yezidis.* (Today much of Nineveh, whose carvings date from the ninth century BC, is under ISIS control.)

Ten more books of archaeology followed, before Layard returned to England, becoming a successful politician and diplomat there.

Venice remained another of his longtime passions. In 1866, Layard founded a glass manufacturing company on the isle of Murano called "Compagnia Venezia Murano," whose London showroom was at 431 Oxford Street. Finally retiring to their beloved Venice in the 1880s, he and Lady Layard moved into the Gothic-style Palazzo Ca' Cappello, which he had purchased in 1874.

His wife, Lady Enid Layard, had grown up on an 11,000-acre estate in Dorset, and had married her archaeologist cousin Henry in 1869, when he was 51 and she was 25. Despite the difference in ages, the marriage was happy, "without a quarrel or a separation of 24 hours!" Enid wrote in her diary after they had been wed a quarter century.

In Venice, the Layards collected early Italian works of art. At their parties, Lady Layard wore a necklace of ancient seals from Mesopotamia, and in their parlor, along with Henry's collection of antiquities, was a portrait of Mahomet II painted in the Ottoman court in 1480 and attributed to Gentile Bellini (1429-1507). (Now in the National Gallery in London, bequest of Lady Enid Layard in 1915.)

When not entertaining in her salon, Lady Enid Layard played the guitar, sculpted, and worked as a volunteer at the Cosmopolitan Hospital on the isle of the Giudecca. Most importantly for today's scholars, for over five decades she kept a diary, whose 14,000 entries filled 8,000 pages.[12] A number of these diary entries mention Evelina, who (for an example) had spent part of a morning with Lady Layard on an "excessively" hot May 28, then returned to the Layards for dinner that evening, remaining in Ca' Cappello until Henry took Evelina home at 10 p.m. On another "splendid moonlit night," the widowed Evelina was again a guest, together with the fascinating Horatio Forbes Brown (of whom more will be discussed shortly).

There were many more evenings with the Layards. As Enid writes in October of 1886, six years after Almorò died, "Countess Evelina Pisani came to see us being in town for a few days." Indeed, by that time Evelina was spending far more time in Vescovana than on the Grand Canal, but when she was in town, she made new friends, including at the Layards' dinner parties. One of these was the American Civil War General George B. McClellan. The two became "great friends"—so say her American friends and neighbors, the Curtises of Boston, in their diary. Years later Evelina would give a birthday dinner for the general's son, 21-year-old George McClellan Jr.

A particularly thrilling Venetian visit took place in October 1889, when the Prince and Princess of Wales steamed down the Grand Canal on their Royal Yacht, the *Osborne*, to a musical fanfare, Roman candles, and Venetian honor guards. Sleeping aboard their yacht, Princess Alexandra and her husband Prince Albert Edward—the future King Edward VII—disembarked to tour the Ducal Palace in Piazza San Marco, and, naturally, to enjoy a luncheon at the Layards, attended by Evelina. Although Evelina had expected these royal Brits for tea at her home, they failed to make it. But they did call in at Palazzo Barbaro, which was, as Prince Albert Edward later confided to Evelina, "the most brilliant" of the private dwellings in Venice—and which happened to be the palazzo in which Evelina lived.

Venice was a favorite of other royals, including Italian. On April 27, 1887, while dining with the Layards once more, "Evelina tried to persuade us to decorate our gondola for the arrival of the K & Q [King Umberto I and Queen Margherita]." A few days later Enid admitted that, alas, to decorate their gondola for the royal visit was simply too expensive, so "we gave up the idea."

As the social royalty of international Venice, a challenge to the Layards came from the wealthy American Katherine De Kay Bronson of New York, who settled permanently in Venice in 1876; her husband, Arthur Bronson, remained behind in Paris, apparently in a home for mental patients. Together with her daughter Edith (who later married into the Florentine nobility, becoming Countess Rucellai), Mrs. Bronson moved into the Palazzino Alvisi, which faces the Church of the Salute across the Grand Canal. She became a doyenne of Venetian society, while also holding classes for the illiterate children of gondoliers.

Katherine Bronson was a distant relation of both James McNeill Whistler (1834-1903) of Lowell, Massachusetts, and of his early patron, railroad builder Thomas de Kay Winans. Whistler had attended the West Point Military Academy, from which he managed to be expelled in 1854, before coming to Europe the following year to study art; he never returned to the U.S. By 1879, after living in England, he was bankrupt and traveled to Venice, where he created a series of etchings and lived for a year. Visiting Katherine Bronson, he declared that, "Venice is only really known in all its fairy perfection to the privileged who may be permitted to gaze from Mrs. Bronson's balcony."[13]

Among those thus privileged was also Don Carlos, pretender to the Spanish throne.

The Bronsons considered their most illustrious visitor to be Robert Browning, a houseguest there with his son, Pen. Browning was already famous for his poem of 1842, "My Last Duchess," which includes these memorable lines:

She had
A heart—how shall I say?—too soon made glad,
Too easily impressed; she liked whate'er
She looked on, and her looks went everywhere.

Browning not only gave readings of his poetry in the Bronson salon, but also dedicated to Katherine his last book of poems, *Asolando*.

At the time, Henry James was a frequent visitor to Venice, and, less celebrated than Browning, was facing something of a crisis in his life. In 1869, he had taken up residence at the Casa Barbesi, returning there with his sister Alice in August of 1872. In 1880, he returned to Venice, this time a lodger in a *pensione* on the Riva degli Schiavoni. Finally, in February 1887, he moved into Casa Alvisi, the guest of Mrs. Bronson and her daughter Edith. He enjoyed his stay there; in a letter to musician Francis Boott in Boston, James said that he was delighted that at the Bronsons' tea parties, "One doesn't hear the clatter of the cup."[14]

While staying with the Bronsons, Henry James also met Evelina for the first time. With almost savage brevity, he described her as: "Widowed, childless, palaced, villaed, pictured, jewelled and modified by Venetian society."[15]

While still a guest of the Bronsons on February 27, 1887, James offered a more lingering description of Evelina in a letter to the American socialite Sarah Butler Wister of Philadelphia. His were not words of faint praise:

The day is lovely—and the golden glow of Venice streams into my room. On laying down my pen yesterday I went out and in the course of the afternoon paid a visit to a most remarkable woman—the Countess Pisani—a lady who vaguely suggests Caterina Cornaro and makes one believe in the romantic heroines of D'Israeli and Bulwer. She has English blood in her veins—her father was the doctor who bled Byron to death at Missolonghi—and her mother a French odalisque out of the harem of the Grand Turk.

By "D'Israeli," James meant, not the British prime minister Benjamin Disraeli, but his father, essayist Isaac D'Israeli, the author of *Curiosities of Literature*, written in 1791 and re-edited by Benjamin for publication in 1881. Bulwer was the English novelist Lord Edward Bulwer-Lytton, author of *The Last Days of Pompeii* (1834), whose heroines were the blind Nydia and Ione, a beautiful and intelligent Greek girl who had to fight off the advances of the cruel sorcerer-seducer Arbaces.

As James went on to say of Evelina,

The late Count Pisani married her thirty-five years ago for her beauty which must have been extraordinary and still is very striking (she is fifty-five and looks about forty); she has spent all her life in Italy ... modified by Venetian society in a kind of mysterious awe—she passes for a great personage and the biggest swell—on the whole—in the place. She is very little in Venice— living mainly at her villa on the mainland, where she farms a large property with un-Venetian energy.

She made an impression—on me—as of one formed of the usual social stuff of today—but the sort of woman one might have found—receiving on a balcony, here—at 2 o'clock on a June morning—in the early years of the century.[16]

James was hardly given to such enthusiasm. Describing about another in the Bronson circle, Princess Olga of Montenegro, he put her down as, "the poor little ineffectual princess with no money or art," who could become in a novel "a possible subject—though it would want filling out and complicating" to make a story.[17]

Another Bronson guest in 1888 was John Addington Symonds (1840-1893), who would become one of Evelina's dearest friends. Symonds, a poet and cultural historian, was a graduate of Balliol College and the author of *Renaissance in Italy*. He was married and the father of four; one of his daughters, Margaret (Madge to her family), born in 1864, would play a significant role in Evelina's life and afterlife as well.

But there was another, deeper story behind Symonds. Living at a time when homosexuality was a criminal offense in his native England, he was not quite secretly gay, although several of his serious love affairs apparently did not involve sex. Throughout the 1800s, the act of sodomy was a felony punishable by imprisonment in England; it was this law which would send Oscar Wilde to prison for two years in 1895. Still, as Symonds wrote in his diary Jan. 28, 1870: "I stripped him naked and fed sight, touch and mouth on these things."[18]

Symonds's book, *A Problem of Greek Ethics* (1883), explored the idea of gay love, though only in ancient Greece, and was printed privately, originally in only ten copies. In a letter to a prospective eleventh reader, Symonds referred to gay relations as "that unmentionable custom," but later he became more open.

For years, he corresponded with Walt Whitman, whose biography Symonds wrote. At one point Symonds tried to prod Whitman into acknowledging homosexual content in *Leaves of Grass* and particularly in the "Calamus" cluster of poems. The calamus root has a vaguely phallic shape, and in these poems, the "manly love of comrades" is celebrated. The word comes from the Greek *kalamos*, moreover, which has a mythical reference to the love between two Greek youths.

Whitman refused Symonds's prodding.[19]

Today, however, Symonds's *Greek Ethics* is considered an important early chapter in gay history, and he is recognized as the first in the English language to have used the word "homosexual" in a book. Today's scholars believe that Venice attracted British homosexual men with the means to travel like John Symonds because, as we read in a groundbreaking essay in *Italian Sexualities Uncovered, 1789-1914*, published in March 2015:

> Venice gave much greater freedom of opportunity than Britain for sexual relationships with other men, but the city also had its own distinct working-class cultures of masculinity, in particular that of the gondoliers, which captured the imaginations of literary homosexual men such as John Addington Symonds and Horatio Forbes Brown. ...
>
> The city of Venice, long associated in the nineteenth century with ruin, former glory and decay, became after 1870 a magnet for a certain kind of foreign artists. [20]

Over time, John Addington Symonds's approach to homosexuality became more bold. Here is one stanza of a poem which he wrote in 1862, called the "Key of Blue," and which was published only three decades later, in 1893:

A gentle youth beside me bent;
His cool moist lips to mine were pressed,
That throbbed and burned with love's unrest:
When, lo, the powers of sleep were spent.

Addressing a conference on "John Addington Symonds and British Masculinity before the First World War," held at Keele University in Staffordshire in September 2010, Dr. Sean Brady of the Universities of Birkbeck and London explained that Symonds's life and writings offer key insights into the difficulties of expressing male homosexuality in Victorian Britain. Symonds's scholarly writings had been "clandestine," said Brady. British society expected conventional marriage, and in Symonds's day, England had a "cultural horror of sex and sexuality between men," to the point that there could be no tolerance even for scholarly or scientific analysis of homosexuality.

Nevertheless, having begun tentatively with his study of Greek male love, Symonds later corresponded extensively with Dr. Havelock Ellis, co-author of the first medical textbook ever written in English on homosexuality, published in 1897. The two men never met. But, according to Dr. Brady, editor of their published correspondence, what Symonds sought was,

... to provide a sympathetic scientific, literary and historical study that did not pathologise sexuality between men and between women. Symonds' writings, his married life, the sexual chastity he maintained with male lovers until he abandoned living in Britain in 1877, provide fascinating and incisive sites of analysis for historicising masculinity and male homosexuality in Britain in the period.[21]

Symonds came to Venice with his wife and two of his daughters, but he was often alone there. His dearest friend in that small but intelligent and worldly circle of foreigners, which had become Evelina's world upon the death of her husband, was Horatio Forbes Brown (1854-1926), a Scot. Together with his mother, in 1879, Horatio rented an apartment in Palazzo Balbi Valier overlooking the Grand Canal, but later purchased, on the quayside embankment called the Zattere, a shabby building, which he had restored. John Symonds and Horatio Brown had been close friends for at least two decades at Clifton College in Bristol, where John was teaching Greek poetry while Horatio was a student there in the 1860s. For many years, every autumn John Symonds spent long periods in Horatio's house on the Giudecca.

Horatio Brown dedicated his first book, *Life on the Lagoons,* to his gondolier, Antonio Salin, "my constant companion in Venice and Venetia." (The book, first published in 1884, has gone through a half dozen editions, the latest published in 2008 by Read Books, London.) Together with his wife and family, Antonio moved into Horatio's home, where Horatio lyrically describes coming unexpectedly upon his gondolier:

I found the door, and at the top of the little staircase there was Antonio, his head fresh from a basin of water, all his masses of hair tossed back and dripping, like Bacchus stepped from Tintoret's loveliest picture, or Saint George with never a dragon left to conquer; a black and white flannel shirt, a blue sash round his waist, a towel in both hands, and his eyes laughing out as he gives the last scrub to his face.[22]

When John Symonds died, his friend in Venice, Horatio Brown, became his literary executor, which required eliminating from Symonds's unpublished texts what Horatio considered dangerous evidence of homosexuality. Years later, Horatio, discussing an obituary of the English writer Frederick Rolfe (another in the Venetian crowd, another with particular interest in young gondoliers, and more openly gay than John Symonds), confessed that: "If it is necessary to modify concerning Rolfe—a freelance with no ties—imagine what I was forced to do in my John Addington Symonds books, with his daughters and their husbands insisting on seeing the MS before it was printed!"[23] (Both Rolfe and Horatio are buried on the Venetian cemetery island of San Michele.)

Brown's editing out of the homoerotic content in Symonds's writings was almost immediately assailed by Edward Carpenter, an English poet who fought in those same years for sexual freedom and recognition that same-sex attraction was normal. Carpenter knew of Symonds; in the 1880s, John Symonds had composed a number of works in defense of same-sex orientation, which were distributed among a small group of people, including Carpenter.

In these society salons in Venice, the real Venetians played a relatively scanty part, to judge by a list of party guests, where the names of the Italians are listed separately from the others.

During their Venice years, Symonds and Brown were swiftly absorbed into those of both the Layards and the Bronsons, and then into a third worldly Venetian salon: that in the city's most magnificent private residence, the historic Palazzo Barbaro, in which Evelina happened to live.

In 1877, the wealthy Daniel Sargent Curtis (1825-1908), his English-born wife, Ariana Wormeley Curtis, and their clever artist son, Ralph, quit Boston to live permanently abroad—first renting in Florence and Rome and then, in 1880, in Venice, where they settled into the Palazzo Barbaro, with a five-year lease prior to their eventual purchase of all but Evelina's portion of the property. In a letter to her sister-in-law in Boston, Mary Curtis, dated Nov. 8, 1885, Ariana Curtis describes the purchase:

> We have bought the Barbaro ... We shall have the whole palace, except Countess Pisani's mezzanine—and pay 70.000 francs—about $13,500 at present rate of exchange. The common Italians are not at all aware of the artistic value of such a unique specimen of decoration of 17th century as our grand sala. They consider the value as based upon the number of rooms, and the vicinity to the Piazza [San Marco]. ... The dining room floor has sunflowers and mother o' pearl.[24]

The top floors only of the building, wrote her husband, had been purchased at "the price of a new brick box on Marlborough Street."

Like other old Venetian noble families, the Barbaros had fallen on hard times. Two fine oval paintings by Ludwig Passini over the doors of the drawing room had been auctioned off in Paris in 1874, a decade before the Curtises purchased the building.

The new owner of the palazzo, Daniel Curtis, was a distinguished Harvard law graduate, who traced his ancestors to their arrival on the Mayflower. Curtis had been a banker and a trustee of the Boston Public Library, but, as many have written, the Curtises had left Boston under a cloud. In his *The City of Falling Angels*, author John Berendt relates one version of the story:

Daniel Curtis was riding in a commuter train from Boston to the suburbs when he got into an altercation with another man over a seat that had been saved for a third party. Words were exchanged. The other man declared that Daniel Curtis was 'no gentleman,' and in reply Mr Curtis twisted the man's nose. The injured party turned out to be a judge, who thereupon brought suit against Daniel Curtis for assault. A trial followed, and Daniel Curtis was convicted and sentenced to two months in jail. Upon his release, according to the story, he indignantly gathered up his family, moved to Europe, and never came back.[25]

In another version, Daniel Curtis is the victim because, gentlemanly, he had insisted that the man who turned out to be a judge give his seat to a pregnant woman.[26]

Whether or not Daniel may have been wronged, the incident took place, and Daniel Curtis had to endure two months in a Boston prison. This, however, does not explain his leaving Boston, for the incident and trial took place a full decade before the family left the United States. What recent biographers believe is that Daniel Curtis and his wife, too, seem to have been seeking a richer cultural context than Boston or, for that matter, any other American city afforded at that time.

For a time, they lived in Florence, where Daniel happened to read John Addington Symonds's study of the Renaissance, which had been published in London in 1879. From Florence, the Curtises came to Venice, where they remained, preserving and restoring almost all of both halves of the magnificent Palazzo Barbaro. Their restoration was so fine that, when the work was complete, Browning tried to coax the now elderly John Ruskin into visiting the palazzo to see it.

Stretching five stories tall and 180 feet wide, the Palazzo Barbaro is actually two conjoined buildings. In the one dating from around 1425 ("good Gothic," as John Ruskin has described it), Isabella d'Este had resided in 1524. The other half, Baroque, dates from 1694.

The Barbaro were among the oldest and wealthiest of Venetian nobles. The family was known from the tenth century, and had grown rich by trading in the salt used to conserve food. Among the early Barbaros on record was Marco, captain of a ship which had fought in the Crusades. In the year 1122, a man later identified as a "Moor" jumped onto the ship and tore down its flag. With his sword, Marco killed the Moor by chopping off his arm. With the bloody stump, he created a new flag by smearing a big white kerchief with the dead man's blood.[27] This broad red circle on a white field became the family's rather disgusting coat of arms. (This Barbaro family crest, gory only if you know its history, is on sale today on a T-shirt for $36.50.)

A later Barbaro, Marcantonio, became a "Procuratore" of San Marco, an office second in importance only to the Doge, in the mid-sixteenth century. Others rose to power in the church and in the military.

The two clans, the Pisani and Barbaro, were distant relations, as was shown by Evelina's wedding in a Barbaro church, but also rivals in self-promotion in their respective deep pasts. Just as Almorò's ancestors in the villa at Strà had Giovanni Battista Tiepolo paint a ceiling that proclaimed the glory of the house of Pisani, around 1750 the Barbaros had the same artist paint the ceiling of their third-floor library with a huge (96" x 183") and boastful "Apotheosis of the Barbaro Family." In it, hard by the main figure, which represents "Valor," is a lion; and behind Valor and Lion stands "Abundance," flaunting a cornucopia. To ensure that the Barbaro family's Valor and Abundance would not go unnoticed, a winged "Fame" hovers overhead, blowing a big trumpet.

Elsewhere in the Palazzo Barbaro were paintings by the noted artists of the baroque, Sebastiano Ricci and Giambattista Piazzetta, gazing down upon walls with gilded boiserie and a showy mosaic pavement that incorporated gleaming tiles of precious mother-of-pearl, as Ariana Curtis had written her sister-in-law in Boston.

At about the time of Evelina's first visit to Venice, the Barbaro Abundance was very much a thing of the past, however. To make ends meet, the Barbaro had their "Apotheosis" sold at auction in Paris in 1874; a half century later (1927), it had made its way into the collection of the Metropolitan Museum in New York. The sale was necessary: following Napoleon's conquest of Venice, this formerly wealthy family found itself in even worse financial straits than the Pisani. So reduced were their circumstances that, not long after Evelina's marriage in their family church, the Barbaro rented out their entire, double palazzo.

It was John Ruskin who recorded that the last two Barbaro brothers—contemporaries of Evelina and Almorò—were miserable wretches holed up in a garret somewhere inside the palazzo the family had occupied for 400 years. For almost a quarter century after Ruskin described the family's pitiful circumstances, the palazzo continued to be sold and resold piecemeal. Its stuccos, sconces, pictures, ornate carved wooden chairs, gilded frames, mirrors, boiseries, and chandeliers were stripped away, one by one, for resale, or left to crumble to dust. Their last survivor, Marcantonio Barbaro, and his wife, Matilde, had no children, and finally sold the entire palazzo in 1858.

By the time the Curtises acquired Palazzo Barbaro, there was a great deal to restore. In the Curtis diary, Ariana described the condition in which they had found the palazzo:

A beam below the 'clerestory' windows has nearly rotted away, from rain having filtered in, and had to be replaced. The wings and feet of many of the stucco putti were broken, apparently children had been allowed to throw hard balls at them, as we found several such on the cornice! Then Mrs. Er had covered the ceiling pictures with bitumen! Saying she did not like faces looking down at her!![28]

On the plus side, between the two buildings, a wall had been smashed through to create a single great hall stretching through both. Otherwise, even after this long hall was cobbled together, the two buildings remained separate.

The palazzo would come to broader public attention when it was used as the setting for *Brideshead Revisited,* the 1981 TV mini-series based on the Evelyn Waugh novel and starring Jeremy Irons. It was also the setting for the 1997 movie of *The Wings of the Dove,* starring Helena Bonham Cartier; curiously, the novel upon which the film was based had been written in part inside that very palazzo, as its author Henry James acknowledged. Indeed, as James also wrote, Palazzo Barbaro was the setting he had "vaguely" imagined for the novel:

> For ... *The Wings,* I had vaguely in mind the Palazzo Barbaro, which you can see very well from the first, the upper, of the iron bridges, the one nearest the mouth of the Grand Canal, and which crosses from Capo San Stefano to the great Museum of the Academy. The palace is the very old Gothic one, on your right, just before you come to the iron bridge.[29]

Almorò had already acquired the mezzanine floor entered by the side canal, the sole portion that would not become Curtis property. In a letter to Alvin Coburn, the photographer who was to take pictures of the settings for Jamesian novels, Henry James described the entryway into that Pisani portion:

> The Barbaro has its water-steps beside it, as it were; that is a little gallery running beside a small stretch of side-canal. But in addition it also has fine water-steps (I remember!) to the front door of the lower apartment. (The side-steps I speak of belong to the apartment with the beautiful range of old upper Gothic windows, those attached to the part of the palace concerned in my story.)

"My story"—*The Wings of the Dove,* and specifically Evelina's portion of Palazzo Barbaro.

The Curtis salon within the restored Palazzo Barbaro attracted many of the same people who congregated at the Layards and Bronsons. There was Horatio Brown and John Symonds; the artist Whistler; the Brownings (as elsewhere, Robert gave readings of his poetry inside the Barbaro); Henry

James; Isabella Stewart Gardner and her husband, Jack; and a young Edith Wharton (1862-1937), who would become a close friend of James. Another visitor was Boston Brahmin Charles Eliot Norton (1827-1908) of Harvard University, the Dante scholar who would one day be Ruskin's literary executor.

These wealthy neo-Venetians moreover acted as benefactors to the dozens of bright young foreign artists who traveled to Venice. They entertained them, subsidized them by collecting their pictures, and had them to tea.

The artist John Singer Sargent, a distant relation of the Bronsons, was also Daniel Curtis's cousin. A frequent guest in Palazzo Barbaro, Sargent enjoyed painting in young Ralph Curtis's studio there. For Venice, said Sargent, taught him "to admire Tintoretto immensely, and to consider him second only to Michelangelo and Titian." In 1898, Sargent would paint "An Interior in Venice," a portrait under the great chandeliers of the ballroom in Palazzo Barbaro of the elder Curtises, their son Daniel, and his wife Lisa. (The painting is now in the Royal Academy in London.)

Like Symonds and Brown, Sargent may have been part of the gay circuit of Venice.

When not painting breathtaking views of Venice, Sargent complained that the city was being spoiled by the "swarms of larky smart Londoners." It is true that tourism to Venice continued to rise. Besides the new steam ships, Western Europe was almost entirely connected by train by 1870. A decade later, steam-powered *vaporetto* boats began to ply the Grand Canal (1881), challenging the power of the gondoliers.

At about the same time came a surge in travel books with beguiling photographic illustrations, including of Venice. Seaside resorts had already existed the previous century, but, with the advent of what has been called "leisure travel" in the late nineteenth century, posh hotels were built on the Venetian Lido and attracted middle class tourists from among those who were newly wealthy, not from land ownership, as in the past, but from industry. These "larky smart" people, who came from the United States as well as North Europe, were among those who for the first time in history were entitled to take holidays, a new concept.

Living inside Palazzo Barbaro, the privileged Contessa Evelina was centerpiece in the cosmopolitan Venetian whirl. She was deeply immersed in the Curtis's circle, as well as in those of the Layards and Bronsons. In addition, her own home became the fourth of the glittering centerpieces of Venetian international society, as Elizabeth Anne McCauley writes in *Gondola Days, Isabella Stewart Gardner and the Palazzo Barbaro Circle*:

With their literary and cultural pretensions, Bostonians were accepted into the Anglo-Saxon network in the city, which centered around the homes of the Curtises, the Bronsons, the celebrated Syrian archaeologist Sir Henry Layard and his younger wife Enid, and the aging, widowed English daughter of Lord Byron's physician the Countess Pisani.[30]

Evelina's portion—the "beautiful rooms on the *piano nobile* of the Palazzo Barbaro"—is described by her then young friend and frequent house guest on the estate at Vescovana, Margaret Symonds, daughter of John Addison Symonds:

They were typical Venetian rooms with long rows of Gothic windows to the drawing-room, and tiny white lions guarding the balconies. Their chief adornment was a great family portrait of Almorò II and his family painted by Pietro Longhi. The town house was fitted up perhaps more sumptuously than that in the country, but it had the same pervading and individual charm. There were lots of mirrors and a little fountain in the drawing-room.[31]

None of those in the widow Evelina's gilded circle of friends was immune from gossip. One critic complained that Evelina had a "hateful character" and had quarreled with everyone in Venice. But Evelina had far more admirers than critics. Shortly after the Curtises arrived in Venice, Henry Layard himself gave them a full rundown on their exotic neighbor, down to and including Evelina's father's presence at Byron's death bed, and her mother Marionca's stay in a harem after marrying a Turkish pasha.

The Curtis diary entry from November 23, 1886, also repeats high praise for Evelina, who was obviously absent from the dining room that evening: "Sir Henry L[ayard] told me he remembers her 40 years ago, very handsome, very clever, speaks English, French and Italian and knows all the literatures. Said Shakespeare's knowledge of Italians was wonderful."

Curiously, the Curtises noted, Evelina had added that, "No Italian woman could be a Lady Macbeth."

Ariana Curtis was an amateur writer, and kept a diary, to which her husband Daniel also contributed. Their diary entry three days later added the details that, besides three Romance languages, Evelina spoke Turkish, German, and Armenian.

In whatever language she spoke, Evelina could be sharp of tongue. In the course of another Palazzo Barbaro dinner party, Evelina herself regaled the Curtises (so they recorded in their diary) with the account of her meeting Lady Anna, the wife of Baron Alan de Tatton Egerton, a member of Parliament for Mid-Cheshire. Immediately after they were introduced, Lady Anna said starchily to Evelina, "You know, in England we don't think much of Italian countesses."

To which Evelina retorted (so she said): "We know, Madame, that you English excel in all things, especially in rudeness."

"Oh, but I don't mean to be rude," said Lady Anna.

"That is just it. You are rude without knowing it."

Needless to say, Evelina's tart reply to Lady Egerton (who may simply have been trying to be funny) was later commented upon by one and all. Out of Evelina's hearing, Lady Egerton later complained that the Contessa Pisani likes inviting friends to dinner well enough, "but only asks those who ask her in return."

By way of reply, Daniel Curtis, showing his agreement with Evelina, said curtly that, "Well, I say 'cutlet for cutlet.'"

Browning, who was not overly fond of Evelina, agreed with Lady Egerton. "That's not my way—I don't feel obliged to ask people in return."[32] In Palazzo Barbaro, Browning would give 25 guests a reading of the poems from *Asolando,* which he dedicated to Mrs. Bronson, on November 19, 1889, just four weeks before he died.

Among the most renowned today of the Curtis circle was Isabella Stewart Gardner (1840-1924), who had first come to Venice in 1883 with her husband, Jack. Throughout the previous year, as Isabella recovered from a miscarriage, the couple had been making a grand tour which had taken them to India, China, Japan, Java, and Cambodia. Their last stop was Venice, where they spent a month in Palazzo Barbaro as guests of the Curtises, whose artist son Ralph Curtis was their friend from Boston.

Isabella had arrived wan and sorrowing (so James described her) from that miscarriage, but became so delighted with the palazzo that from 1884 on the Gardners rented a portion of it for several months every other summer for eight years.[33] Isabella took particular delight in the fact that Palazzo Barbaro was near the Accademia Bridge, for, as she said, from it she could stroll to the museum to study its collection of Old Masters.

While visiting Boston in 1888, Sargent painted Isabella's portrait, which is now in the museum she created there. The two, Sargent and Mrs. Gardner (or Mrs. Jack, as she was often known) had been introduced by Henry James; and some critics believe that Mrs. Gardner was among the possible women who inspired the portrait of Milly Theale in *The Wings of the Dove,* part of which James wrote during one of his long stays in Palazzo Barbaro, but which was published only in 1902.

Evelina already knew both Isabella Stewart Gardner and Henry James. Now, with James a guest of the Curtises in Palazzo Barbaro, both were her next-door neighbors. Together they enjoyed at Evelina's home, as well as at the Curtises, dinners and tea parties (one hopes without clattering cups).

One who had slipped past Evelina on the social circuit was John Ruskin. Hoping to meet him, one day in 1888, Evelina sat down and wrote him a letter asking to make his acquaintance. Ruskin, by then 69 years old, replied that he was obliged to decline her kind invitation, "probably on grounds of ill health," the Curtises noted graciously, adding, however, with a hint of venom, that a publisher in Berlin had sent Ruskin a copy of Evelina's mother's "curious" book about life in a harem.

But Evelina was not one to be discouraged. Ignoring that Ruskin had brushed her off, "la Pisani came, saw & conquered Ruskin, who had declined to see her." (So reads a Curtis diary entry dated Oct. 15, 1888.) Arriving in Venice from the estate at Vescovana,

> She compelled [underscore in the original] Horatio Brown to go with her to Ruskin's hotel, where their names were sent up & he received them. She told us all they said (which we had heard from Brown but did not say so). She praised his books, quoted, talked of Tommaso Mocenigo, and gave him [Ruskin] a gold medal of the Pisani doge.

On occasion, she was less socially successful. Four days later, Evelina coaxed the Curtises into presenting her to "Mr. Browning," who was living in the towering baroque palazzo he had purchased, Ca' Rezzonico, which dated from 1667. At that dinner party, where Robert Browning dwelled at length about his youthful admiration of Shelley, "Mr. Browning and *la Pisani* did not take to each other. He said afterwards that that lady could be malignant," wrote one of the Curtises in a penciled postscript. (Popular with tourists today, Ca' Rezzonico houses the Museum of Eighteenth Century Venice.)

For the Curtises, Browning was the greatest show on earth, and their most important guest, whose every doing they chronicled. By contrast, James was always identified as "Henry James, author," which presumes that otherwise no one would know who he was. They even called him, *patronizingly*, "poor Henry," who "now looks like a kind cardinal, doesn't he?" After seeing him in London, they wrote: "I had tea with Henry James at his club for one and a half hours. Nitroglycerine (really) always in his waistcoat pocket, alone. Tides him along."[34]

Although Henry James did not usually stay long in Venice, he visited it frequently. He was just 25 when he first came to Italy in 1869, when he noted about Venice that, "There is nothing more to be said about it."[35] As James also wrote in 1882, "Venice has been painted and described many thousands of times, and of all the cities in the world is the easiest to visit without going there. Open the first book and you will find a rhapsody about it, step into the first picture dealer's and you will find three or four high-colored views of it."

Having written that there was nothing more to say about Venice, James went on to write thousands of pages about Venice, either as descriptions of the city and its arts or as an emotional backdrop to his novels.

The first, in which he mentions John Ruskin five times on page one, was his *Venice: An Early Impression*, first published in 1872. Did he like Ruskin? Not particularly at that time, at least. "An hour on the lagoon is worth a hundred pages of [Ruskin's] demoralized prose," James decreed. As for Ruskin's *Stones of Venice*, said James, "it appears addressed to children of tender age. It is pitched in the nursery key," as if "written by an angry governess."[36] (Later he acknowledged that "there is no better writer" on Venice than Ruskin.)[37]

May 1887 found James again in Venice, intending to stay ten days as a guest of the Curtises in Palazzo Barbaro. Instead he lingered there for five weeks. He had arrived ashen-faced and ill, but, given a suite of cool rooms at the back of the palazzo overlooking the garden, he could not bring himself to leave, as he admitted. It was the longest he had ever stayed as a guest in a "private family," he wrote Grace Norton on July 23, 1887.[38] He was delighted to be there.

> If in the absence of its masters you have happened to have it [Palazzo Barbaro] to yourself for twenty-four hours you will never forget the charm of its haunted stillness, late on a summer afternoon for instance, when the call of playing children comes in behind from the campo, nor the way the old ghosts seem to pass on tiptoe on the marble floors.[39]

From the palazzo, he mailed to his publisher the final version of *The Aspern Papers*.

Here, from a letter from James to an American friend Catherine Walsh in 1887:

> I have been paying a long visit—long for me, who likes less and less as I grow older, to stay with people—to the Daniel Curtises, formerly of Boston but who have been living here for years and are the owners of this magnificent old palace—all marble and frescoes and portraits of Doges—a delightful habitation for hot weather ... she and her husband are very intelligent, clever and hospitable people.[40]

At the time of another of James's Venetian visits, during the summer of 1892, the Curtises had rented their palazzo to Isabella Stewart Gardner. Mrs. Jack had filled every room with guests, and so turned over to James the opulent, airy library on the top floor. This "divine old library," as he described it, decorated with eighteenth century *chinoiserie*, had been outfitted for him with a four-poster bed draped with netting against the mosquitos James complained about. Still, he emoted over the view from its window, and slowly fell in love with the palazzo, "a place of which the full charm only sinks into your spirit as you go on living there seeing it in all its hours and phases," as James wrote later.

At the same time, James was not blind to the plight of the real Venetians, who included the children with "hungry little teeth ... very nearly as naked as savages." Their little bellies "protruded like those of infant cannibals."[41]

Scholars analyzing James's work focus on his female heroines, who are always unusual, vibrant, and different. Many have speculated about who the models were for these heroines. Isabella Stewart Gardner may have been one, as was his late cousin Mary ("Minny") Temple, who died of tuberculosis in 1879 at age 24.

Another possible prototype was Constance Fenimore Woolson (1840-1894), a prolific writer of popular fiction originally from Cleveland, and grand-niece of James Fenimore Cooper. The two had met in Venice in 1880, and James admired her immensely.[42] Their friendship was all the more important because, as we are told, during that decade James was frustrated and unhappy. Of their friendship, *New York Times* critic Brooke Allen has written:

> The fertile creative period from *Daisy Miller* to *The Portrait of a Lady* had ended, and all three major novels of the decade were commercial flops. Woolson, on the other hand, was on something of a roll, and the success she achieved with her serious novels and stories for the better magazines was of a type James can only have envied.[43]

Apparently to buck up James, Woolson wrote him that, "Even if a story of mine should have a large 'popular' sale, that could not alter the fact that the utmost best of my work cannot touch the hem of your first or poorest. ... I do not come in as a literary woman at all, but as a sort of—of admiring aunt."[44]

In 1893, Woolson moved into an elegant apartment she had rented on the Grand Canal. Not long afterward she died, an apparent suicide when she fell to her death from a third-floor window onto the pavement beside a lesser canal. That death on January 24, 1894, which was presumably caused by depression, turned James himself against Venice. (Woolson is buried in the Protestant Cemetery in Rome, which a grieving James visited; it had been, coincidentally, the graveyard for his fictional character Daisy Miller in the novel of that name, published in 1879.)

There can be no doubt that Woolson played a huge role as exemplary of the type of woman James admired. But, as we have seen, he had also come to admire Evelina in an extraordinary way, to the point that, before turning his back on Venice, James would travel to Vescovana for a three-day visit to that "lady who vaguely suggests Caterina Cornaro and makes one believe in the romantic heroines of D'Israeli and Bulwer."

Triumph

In their early years of marriage, Evelina and Almorò had myriad distractions from their social life in Venice. They made long and pleasant sojourns to Vescovana, where Almorò tended to the property management and to his friends in a horse club and a Masonic lodge at nearby Padua.

While she was in what they called their "Sunday house," Evelina read and studied languages, embroidered needlepoint, was entertained by her pet monkey, and took solitary drives in a pony cart through the alternately sun-bleached and water-logged countryside. They also traveled abroad, making a long visit the year after they were married to Constantinople to see Julius, and then holidays in England, Paris, and, to escape the Venetian summer heat, the Alpine resorts of San Moritz, Pontresina, and the Engadine.

But duty also called them regularly from Venice to Vescovana, where the Pisani estate lay between the towns of Padua and Rovigo in the Bassa Padovana, as the Veneto flatlands are known. The 37-mile trip via gondola, steam train, and horse-drawn carriage took them five hours.

Originally, these outlying estates of the Venetian nobles had served as a form of defense for Venice itself, and in fact the property had been owned by the Pisani since 1468, when they purchased it at auction in Venice from the Este family. The house was constructed atop the ruins of a late medieval fortress, traces of whose foundation stones have been found. At that time of its purchase, the Pisani property extended to include four towns: Vescovana, Stanghella, Boara, and Solesina. The manor house itself was outsized, extending to 70,000 square meters (753,000 sq. ft.), which made it extremely difficult to manage and maintain.

After the early times, the Venetian nobles maintained estates like Almorò's in order to generate income, even though this was not always assured given the uncertainty of the weather and the risk of flooding. Every springtime, their land, bordered by a canal and squeezed between the Adige and the Gorzone Rivers, risked becoming engorged with run-off water from the Alps to the north. As a preventive measure, as is documented, Almorò's Pisani ancestors in the sixteenth century had begun an ambitious project of draining the soggy marshland, in order to create fertile acres where they grew grains, citrus fruits, and tobacco.

Still, an inventory of 1617 provides a somewhat shocking description of the land, with just "777 good fields" as opposed to 431 fields that were "sinking" and 320 completely submerged under water. The house, however, was elaborately decorated with fine frescoed ceilings in the 1550s by Cardinal Alvise Pisani. It was then when it was described as a "*casa domenicale*" or "Sunday house," the affectionate term Almorò and Evelina used for it.

Almorò inherited the estate in 1850, only three years before their marriage. At that time, every aspect of it was in sore need of improvement. Construction of the newer runoff canals had not yet been entirely paid, and Almorò had to devote considerable time to the banks as well as to his bailiffs, as the overseers were called. The house had gradually been elongated with wings for stables and dovecotes, to the point that it had become as long as Piazza San Marco in Venice. It was large enough that, while the Veneto was under Austrian rule, and Evelina was visiting her Austrian friends in Venice, no less than 200 soldiers and their horses were billeted in the house.

Its grandiosity continued to make its management difficult. The house rose three stories tall, but when Evelina first arrived, only the ground floor was livable. At that time, the top story was still used for grain storage, and hence was overrun by rats, whose nightly capers frightened the occasional guest trying to sleep in bedrooms below. Until Evelina introduced change, even the grand reception room on the ground floor, or *piano nobile*, was piled with firewood. Beans lay drying in baskets, and, beneath the ceiling frescos by Renaissance artists Giovanni Battista Zelotti and Dario Varotari (both students of Veronese), laundry dangled from lines drawn across the room.

Over the door, which exited to the north side and toward the miniscule village, was a date, 1613, presumably indicating the last renovation before Evelina's day. This main door led directly into the triangular-shaped village piazza, with its church and bell tower, where a farmer's market was held every Friday.

Again, until Evelina's time, the front and back doors of the house were often left open, providing a shortcut for farm workers walking from fields to church or market. On occasion a pig also wandered through, or even hopped onto a ruined old parlor sofa to doze on the frayed silk covers. The rooms were also visible from outside, and on occasion farmers returning home from pasturing their animals could peer through the low windows to see the Count and Countess seated at table and dressed grandly for dinner.

That rear door facing south gave onto nothing but "barren ground," according to a description in an early "state of tithe" accounts book. When Evelina first came to Vescovana, only one small pear tree and a single rose bush stood outside that door. However, entry was gained via a broad stone staircase, which was flanked on either side by a handsome stone balustrade, capped with decorative little pyramids.

After five years of marriage, Evelina began to concentrate upon improvements in the house as well as the garden. First, she tackled the northern entry into the village square, pushing back its frontage to create privacy, and installing a wrought-iron gate that kept both workmen and pigs out of the parlor.

On the opposite, southern side, she had the stone staircase torn down so as to create space for a broad, low terrace, from which the enlarged new garden she was excogitating, with formal geometrical plan, would be seen. Into the new garden went the decorative stone balustrades stripped from the old staircase. The lone pear tree remained and prospered. As the years went by, so did the garden, which continued to expand with ample space for statues, fountains, and a fish pond. Shrubs were planted to border gravel paths, and beds planted for flowers—iris, syringa, water lilies in the pond, and, especially, tulips.

Evelina's inspiration for the new garden came from one of the drawings published in *Hortus Floridus* by the brilliant Dutch horticulturist Crispijn van de Passe (1589-1670); and indeed, Evelina, who liked giving places names as if they were her children, christened that first and most prominent section of her garden "Crispin de Pass."

She also drew upon the book *The Formal Garden in England*, by Edwardian architect Sir Reginald Blomfield (1856-1942). Albeit English, Blomfield promoted a return to the traditional Dutch garden of the seventeenth century, and indeed Evelina's tulip bulbs were ordered, not from Holland, but from a Mr. Barr in England, "who has sent me no end of bulbs, and for two days I have not been out of the garden," as she wrote a friend.

Continuing to follow Blomfield's advice, she also introduced manicured topiary shrubs.

Keeping company with these English and Dutch garden references were her recollections of the formal Italianate garden at Villa Torlonia, which she had come to know while she was a schoolgirl in Rome. And indeed, many of the figures and fountains she chose to have scattered throughout the Villa Pisani garden harked back to Rome. There were statues of tritons, or the mythical Greek sea messengers also known as mermen; a typically Baroque fountain with a backing of a stone seashell; a pissing Dionysian satyr; and twisted columns as if from Roman antiquity.

At the same time, there were exotic references to the Islamic culture of Constantinople, where the garden traditionally represents paradise. Reflecting this garden culture were four stone peacocks with iron crests, two of them standing upon the stone balustrade by the vine-draped trellis; in Byzantine garden lore, the peacock represented immortality. From a central fountain (one of two large fountains), paths divided the garden into the four traditional

Islamic garden areas representing earth, water, air, and fire. Elsewhere she dubbed a section the "Temple of Baal," for the Satanic figure also known as Beelzebub, who appears in Greek and Roman legend as well as in Hebrew texts and the Koran.

In a reference to Alpine meadows, Evelina created a stone mountain garden. Traditionally called a rockery, she ironically named this one the "Mockery," the joke being that her land was infinitely flat. Seeking appropriate plants for it, she and friends scoured the nearby slopes of the Euganean Hills.

By the time it was completed, Evelina's garden, replete with theater as well as the chapel, would cover no less than fourteen acres, in a unique mingling of Italian, English, Dutch, and Turkish horticultural traditions. To have created this during her brief periods away from their social life in Venice was already to deal with a huge variety of problems—the immense house, the formal garden. But she took delight in the garden, her creation, her child.

Her husband's death dramatically altered Evelina's lifestyle. For the 27 years of their marriage she had devoted herself to the improvements in the house and to construction of her now huge and elegant garden. Bereft of Almorò, she had little choice but to become manager of the farming portion of the estate, as well as of the formal garden.

She felt ill-prepared for such a demanding project. Writing to her friend, Margaret Symonds (1869-1925), who was the daughter of John Addington Symonds, Evelina summed up her life in what strikes the outside reader as extremely modest terms:

> I wish I were not so old, stupid and ignorant, but I cannot help it. I feel as though I were not up to the mark, and I vainly try to improve. … The fact is all my masters got tired of me; they found me too stupid. That accounts for my extreme ignorance and incapacity for doing anything well. …
>
> There are also persons of my sort whom one might call '*une stupide intelligente.*' This used to make me miserable, but now I get reconciled to my lot, and feel very thankful that I can enjoy the intelligence of other people.

While beginning the mammoth undertaking of managing the estate, Evelina had the almost life-sized statue of Almorò placed inside the chapel. Then, in front of the large central fountain in her garden, visible from the terrace at the south door, she had a rectangular flower bed built which spelled out the name ALMORO.

On a less sentimental level, now that her sole income came from the farmland at Vescovana, its earnings were expected not only to provide her with an income, but also to complete repayment of the last of the mortgages placed upon the property. She alone was responsible for those mortgages, as well as for the immense house, for the vast acreage of farmland, and for the 400 tenant farmers who tilled their allotments.

As a result, not surprisingly, Evelina spent ever less time in international high society Venice. As her Venetian friends remarked in whispers, Evelina's estate was far from in good order. Before the city-dwelling rich Curtises, formerly of Boston, had ever visited Vescovana, they gave the Vescovana property a terrible review based upon gossip from other friends. In a diary entry dated November 23, 1886, no less than six years after Almorò died, Ariana Curtis wrote that the Contessa Pisani is now living an hour from Padua, in "flat, ugly country, hot or cold or foggy ... There her husband is buried & [she] 'promised not to leave him'—so stays there alone ... "

Three days later, Evelina had abandoned her peasants briefly to return to Venice, where she dined next door as Curtis guests in Palazzo Barbaro. That evening, the Curtises gleaned a few more details about her life in the country, again faithfully recorded in their diary: "Dining with us she said she owns and tills some 3,000 acres with 400 peasants near Padova in a flat ugly country, often under water, growing wheat & grano Turco [corn or maize], but no vines [grapes]."

Almost as an aside, Mrs. Curtis acknowledged that, "She is still handsome in Paris toilette and many pearls: altogether a brilliant person: but never liked by the old Venetians."[2]

None of this was easy, but Evelina was intelligent and had developed a will power of steel. What Evelina did not tell the Palazzo Barbaro circle was that, trusting no one, fully aware of how alone she was at Vescovana, she slept with a highly polished, loaded pistol dangling from a peg beside her bed. She also maintained her privacy when checking on the separate farms of which the estate was composed by now riding in an enclosed horse-drawn carriage.

In rebuilding the estate, Evelina imported English mowing machines. She had barns reconstructed with airy, high ceilings, and clean stalls. Hers was hands-on management, and, when in a barn she once saw a calf half-strangled by a rope, she personally leaped into a stall in order to free it.

On first taking charge of the estate, Evelina found that she had just 20 white oxen to plough her 3,000 acres, whereas the norm was for 20 oxen to work 120 acres, meaning that she had just 1/25 of the oxen necessary. On the positive side, hers were of a fine breed, which helped her to build up a model herd, to the point that within a few years she had 500 healthy oxen. Many of these she recognized fondly. Typical of her, she gave them names: Homer, Gladstone, Roma, Tennyson, and, for the most impressive bull, Magnifico.

As this suggests, despite the extraordinarily heavy work load, Evelina did not lose her sense of humor. Teasingly she called the estate "Gromboolia," after the verse called "The Dong with a Luminous Nose", written by Victorian poet Edward Lear (1812-1888). The name comes from its first (and slightly ominous) stanza:

When awful darkness and silence reign
Over the great Gromboolian plain,
Through the long, wintry nights:
When the angry breakers roar...

However long the winter nights, however angry the breakers on her Gromboolian plain, within twelve years of her sole ownership, Evelina had created what was by then recognized as a model farm. She had triumphed.

No one has painted a more thorough portrait of Evelina's successful life on what became that astonishingly model farm than Margaret Symonds, the daughter of John Addington Symonds. Margaret's first visit to Vescovana took place in May of 1888, when she was just 19, and Evelina, 58. Margaret traveled there together with her father and with Horatio Brown and his mother. Two Venetian gondoliers also accompanied them, one of whom was surely Brown's intimate friend Antonio.

In the course of four years, Margaret spent other long visits at Vescovana with Evelina, who came to think of Margaret as an adoptive daughter and indeed named a garden section after her. (Margaret's fascinating account of those visits, the 288-page *Days Spent on a Doge's Farm*, was first published in New York in 1893 and is still available for purchase, digitalized and reprinted recently by the University of California Libraries.)

Following her first visit to "Gromboolia" in 1888, on the basis of her hostess's account of it, Margaret described the house as Evelina had first seen it:

> The great long villa stood bare and flat upon the plain. No single tree shielded it from the baking sun of summer, no flower-bed was there to strengthen the buds of spring ... The garden consisted of square plots of earth, edged in with box. Its principal features were two huge threshing-floors in front of the dining room windows.

It is natural, Margaret concluded, that her "strong English instinct" had made Evelina shudder at such a sight, and set out to build her fine garden, now surrounded by handsome stands of magnolia, poplar, and chestnut trees.

Young Margaret's own focus was primarily botanical: the farming in the area—its crops, its flowers, its trees. But a preface to an edition published after Evelina's death, and two decades after Margaret's first visit to Vescovana, contains intimate letters received from Evelina which Margaret felt she could not publish during Evelina's lifetime. In these letters, wrote Margaret in the new preface, Evelina was occasionally caustic; her pen "was rather more of a weapon than a friend—it was a sharp, incisive tool."[3]

In this preface to the second edition, a perhaps by then forgetful Margaret (her nickname was Madge)—19 at the time of her first visit, pushing 50 at the time of the reprint in 1908—explained that before that first visit to Vescovana, her father and Evelina had never previously met, although Evelina "knew and had long loved my father through his books." This is an error: by that time the two, Evelina and John Addington Symonds, had known each other for at least a year.

Their meeting, at any rate, amounted to "a sort of fairy-tale episode in our Venetian life," Margaret enthused. "I instantly felt that I was in the presence of a great personality."[4] Venetian society was "in no ways intellectual at that period," and, in her opinion, Evelina was too spirited to fit in very well there. Writing with only small exaggeration, Margaret concluded that,

> She found that the large spaces and repose of the old farmhouse upon the mainland suited better with her deeper tastes; her husband also preferred that life, and more and more they [had] lived at Vescovana, the young wife spending ever longer periods among her books and flowers, for neighbours practically did not exist. ... She has often described to me the immense length of the days, and the yards of embroidery with which she filled the gaps.[5]

But the shared yet solitary life of books and flowers and embroidery was in the beginning. In taking over management of the estate, Margaret went on to say, the widowed Evelina made efforts to see that the "peasants" for whom she was now responsible were healthy and well fed.[6] She concerned herself with every detail of farm life, down to and including schooling, and, later, possible love matches among the children of the farm workers. She tended to the oxen, but also to the batches of kittens found in the corner of a barn. She enlisted the elderly local parish priest, Don Antonio Mugna, as her bookkeeper and confidante.

In her letters to Margaret, Evelina registered a few complaints. "How difficult it is to understand the peasants!" Evelina wrote in one letter. "They reason like children, and when you are kind to them they act like spoilt children." After seeing a pitched battle take place between two angry farm worker crews who attacked each other with knives and pitchforks, an exasperated Evelina wrote, "Such black beards and ferocious faces you never saw but in the Middle Ages!"[7]

Local authorities and her bailiffs often struck her as obtuse. In yet another letter to Margaret, Evelina complained that, "When I have discussed for some time with these men I am perfectly exhausted—I cannot write nor read, and I go round the garden to gather new thoughts and new strength."[8]

Her tenant farmers had their own complaints. One was that she had confiscated a tenant's chickens after becoming convinced that he was stealing her grain. Poverty was the norm—poverty and the deadening repetition of the workload, season after season. Moreover, these men with black beards and ferocious faces lived with their wives and children in wretched dwellings. From Margaret Symonds comes this description of the home of one of the farmers:

> The most miserable mud hut can be entered at any time of the day. Its big bed, stuffed with the husks of maize, will be spotlessly clean and smoothly made, although hens may be running under it, and the turkeys sitting in baskets by its side. There will not be a cinder on the hearth, save in the exact middle, where a neat pile of sticks crackle under the pot of polenta; and however poor the inhabitants, there will surely be a good show of burnished copper pails or platters along the wall.
>
> Yet at this point any description of pleasing objects has to cease. The house is usually composed of two to three rooms on the basement—upper storeys are abhorred by the native—its walls painted white, and usually composed of mud and reeds, the roof made of thatch, and not a flower or a creeper to brighten the eternal vista of corn or maize.

Not surprisingly, these farm workers did not understand why Evelina would plant, instead of useful food crops, flowering sweet peas (*Lathyrus odoratus*) solely for decoration.

With Evelina ever more permanently residing at Vescovana, relief from country life came via the constant flow of distinguished guests. Most stayed several days, distracting a delighted Evelina from her accounts, her beloved white oxen, her five big white Maremma sheep dogs, the crude bailiffs, and the ever-frustrating local officials.

In 1886, when Evelina had been a widow for six years, these guests at last included the Layards. Then came Robert Browning, the Symonds father and daughter, and the Curtis's son Ralph. Writing to Isabella Stewart Gardner in November of 1888, the young artist reported that he had made a whole tour of grand Veneto estates. "I have been staying with the Morosinis, Rombos, Pisanis and Marcellos at the villas, which are far more civilized than I had supposed, and their society is queer and amusing to study."[9]

During one of the more bucolic moments in the autumnal countryside of the Bassa Padovana, Henry James came to Vescovana for a visit of three days. Before his arrival, Evelina was concerned enough that she asked Ariana Curtis, who was to accompany James, to bring along a butler to tend the author.

In the event, as Ariana Curtis's account of his visit confirms, Evelina at 56 continued to enchant James, despite the fact that he was far removed from the bucolic world depicted in this entry from the Curtis diary:

In June '87 we spent 3 days at Pisani's Estate at Vescovana ... by rail together with the Marchesa Gavotti-Verospi, wife of the master of ceremonies at the Court of Rome, & her two daughters. Countess P[isani] also asked us to bring our servant, Angelo, to wait on Henry James (the author staying with us) and me. House & outbuildings of immense length - & covered with roses, with plantations, to a chapel where statue of Almorò P[isani]. Drove over Estate with barns etc., 300 superb white oxen—perfect neatness. Tea in model cottage, 100 peasants, men & women in Sunday dress drawn up in two files for our inspection & a glass of wine.

At the harvest gleaning H[oratio]. F. Brown saw the Pisani arrive at the fields in cart covered in red & gold, drawn by 6 white oxen caparisoned, where 500 women gleaners waited her signal to follow. This idea I suggested when there: that she should do Ceres. She said, I will, & she did. Her stately beauty & *port-de-reine* [queenly carriage] which well carry it off. What subject for Troyok [Tolstoy?] Her chaplain, Don Antonio, should have been Harcopex in white & gold [Haruspex, the ancient Roman priest who divined entrails].

The following year, the Layards were at Vescovana. It was early in November of 1888, and Lady Layard's diary entry illustrates the autumnal entertainments.

Packed & started for Vescovana after an early lunch. Mrs Brown [Horatio's mother?] met us at the station & we took charge of her. Mr Brown saw her off but did not go. We went by train to St Elena. Unfortunately it was a wet day & the weather looked bad for our visit. Carriages were waiting for us on our arrival & after about ½ hour's drive we got to the Villa & were received a bra ouverts [with open arms] by Countess Pisani. She gave us tea in her beautiful sala & then she & I sat & gossiped in her boudoir. At 7.30 we dined & D[on]. Antonio the old priest was there. We were a very merry party. Music & patience in the evening.

The following morning, November 3, Lady Layard wrote:

We each had our first breakfasts in our rooms. The weather was splendid. The girls who were in the room next us, picked grapes out of their window from the pergola & Ola breakfasted out on the balcony. When I was dressed I went in to Countess Pisani who having a bad cold was still in bed where she had been doing "un po' di conti con gli uomini" [some accounting with her men], as her maid said. ... In the evening Miss de Bunsen & Ola played the piano & Henry played patience.

The very next day, as a surprise, the Curtises—who had earlier given a sour review of the Vescovana estate to their dinner guests—also appeared, the Countess having invited them by telegraph.

We had a very lively dinner & much joking & laughing. In the evening music ... The next day was sunny, and the country revels continued with a visit to the stables.

It was a very pretty sight to see 4 ploughs & 32 white oxen at work at the same time. We visited the calves & fed them with pumpkins & then went to the stables to see those who were in & also a pretty little calf born two days ago who out of compliment to Henry is to be called Nimroud.

To Evelina, the visitor most important of all was the Empress of Germany, who happened to be the eldest daughter of Queen Victoria. Named for her queenly mother, the Empress too was named Victoria, but was more commonly known as the "Empress Frederick," for her late husband, German Emperor Frederick III. The two women, Evelina and the Empress, had much in common: both were widows, both beautiful, and both English (so Evelina had come to consider herself in her later years).

Upon the death of his father at age 90, William I, on March 9, 1888, the 57-year-old Frederick had succeeded as Emperor of Germany and King of Prussia. Many in Europe had long admired both Frederick and his wife Victoria, for by the standards of their day they were considered liberal, and Frederick had famously disagreed with the aggressive policies of Chancellor Otto von Bismark. However, before his own policies could be implemented, Frederick died on June 15, 1888, after just 99 days on the throne.

His death triggered a firestorm in the German press, for well before Frederick was elevated to emperor and king he had been diagnosed with cancer of the larynx. His German physicians disagreed about what was to be done: one urged a tracheotomy, another said that simply inserting a tube into his throat would suffice and help him breathe. In the event, the tube was chosen but was badly inserted, worsening his condition by causing an abscess. As a result, by the time Frederick succeeded to the throne, he was already unable to speak, and could communicate only through written messages.

In hopes of saving him, the German doctors summoned the most prestigious throat specialist in Europe, Sir Morrell Mackenzie, who arrived from Windsor for a consultation. Mackenzie determined that no operation was required, and the tumor remained. When Frederick died only shortly afterward, the German press pilloried Mackenzie for ineptitude.

A few months after the Emperor died, a deeply troubled Mackenzie arrived in Venice, traveling incognito with his son and daughter. He was in search of a suitable future residence for the new widow, Victoria, he explained. He had first considered Rome, but dismissed it as "too much of a Court." By contrast, Venice seemed perfect for "the most perfect woman" he had ever known, the Empress Frederick.

In Venice, the visibly worn Sir Mackenzie was immediately drawn into the protective society of the usual international set. As it happened, he was an old friend of the Layards, and Lady Layard noted in her diary that tending the emperor on his deathbed must have been difficult, for Sir Mackenzie appeared "thinner & his eyes deeper & larger after his long service with the Emperor & the furious attacks of the German Press." Still, he attended a tea party offered by Isabella Stewart and Jack Gardner, just then tenants in Palazzo Barbaro. Among the guests were Evelina, Robert Browning, and his son, Pen.

Despite his personal problems, Venice enthralled Sir Mackenzie, who encouraged the Empress herself to visit the following year. Dressed in black widow's weeds, she arrived in Venice on October 20, 1889, with her two princess daughters and a robust entourage of servants. The city authorities awaited her arrival at the Venice train station, where soldiers stood honor guard and a band played in front of a vast crowd of the curious. As the Empress and her suite were wafted down the Grand Canal in grand gondolas, oared by gondoliers in scarlet livery, hundreds of Venetians lined the way and hung over the bridge parapets to watch in thrall. "The Empress looked pleased and happy," Ariana Curtis noted in her diary.

While she was in Venice, the Empress became fast friends with Evelina. The following autumn, accompanied by her two daughters and, presumably, several servants, she returned to the Veneto September 22, 1890, for a three-day visit. To welcome her to Vescovana, Evelina, who was by then 59 years of age, had the German flag hoisted on a pole from a balcony of her house. The Empress responded by bestowing upon Evelina a diamond encrusted brooch.

A painting by Ludwig Passini shows Evelina and an unnamed female friend seated in Palazzo Pisani, where Evelina would have received the Empress. Despite the fact that this was a great hall with painted ceilings, the atmosphere is intimate, and colored by Evelina's memories of Constantinople. By the sofa where the two ladies are seated in the painting are two small tables inlaid in ivory; on one are Turkish slippers. Turkish style, the ladies' feet rest upon big soft brown cushions, rather than on the floor, which is covered with Turkish carpets. The windows behind are hung with velvet draperies in burgundy and sheer silk curtains in pink.

In its way, this royal visit was a culmination of Evelina's life. She had overcome every obstacle. As a child she had accepted her grandmother, the Church in Rome, and the absence of her father and mother. During her years in Constantinople she had learned to respect the Islamic culture. As a bride in Venice she had adjusted to the demands of high society—and then to the loneliness of widowhood. She had devoted herself to her workers in the Veneto and had come to understand and to admire country life even though it sometimes left her "melancholy," as she had admitted to Margaret Symonds.

For Evelina, the Empress's visit marked a personal triumph.

Or so it seemed until Evelina's past rose up to haunt her once again.

9

Tulips

The tulips are too excitable, it is winter here.
Look how white everything is, how quiet, how snowed-in.
I am learning peacefulness, lying by myself quietly
As the light lies on these white walls, this bed, these hands,
I am nobody.

Sylvia Plath, 1960

Evidently the Empress's visit to Vescovana was widely publicized before it took place, for, apparently out of nowhere, Evelina's errant brother Frederick suddenly reappeared at Vescovana. Since he had been ousted from Venice at Almorò's intervention so many years before, the wild and extremely prolific Frederick had published a great deal. He literally churned out pamphlets and books: *Wild Life Among the Koords* (1870), *Turkey under the Reign of Abdul-Aziz* (1862), and two anti-Semitic tracts in French and German (1870 and 1873, respectively).

However eccentric, in 1870 Frederick was sufficiently regarded that at a meeting of the Anthropological Society of London he had presented a paper entitled *Slavery in Turkey, The Sultan's Harem*, given a brief review in the daily London *Standard*.

More books followed: *Les Imams e les derviches: pratiques, superstitions et moeurs des Turcs* (1881); *Women in Turkey* (1886); *Revelations about the Assassination of Alexander II* (1886); *The Russians in 1877-78, War in the East* (1889), and more besides.

Despite his long list of publications, Frederick was never out of debt. Creditors had been haunting him from the time that he had lived in London before moving to Paris. As he explained in one of his books,

Our landlord [in London] was the hairdresser to the Prince of Wales and to Mussurus Pasha, the Turkish Ambassador. My enemies were therefore able to approach him [the hairdresser], make him their emissary, and pit him against me. After several scenes between us two, my mother decided to take the debt upon herself in order to extricate me.

His mother failed to extricate him, however, and for seven months Frederick fought off the bailiffs. In the end, using one of his aliases, Frederick was forced to steal away from England on an outward-bound ship.

Evelina had had no contact with Frederick since 1882, two years after Almorò's death, when he had brought a lawsuit against her, evidently in hopes of squeezing money from the (presumably) rich widow. Now, arriving at Vescovana at the time of the Empress's visit, he was plainly spying on her, the royal princesses, and on his sister. He later wrote of his disgust at sight of the German flag flying in front of the villa:

> It darkened the light and stifled the breathing of the amazed peasants.
>
> The Vescovana police were summoned to protect the Contessa Pisani and, not least, her illustrious guests, and expelled Frederick.
>
> The servile police gave me orders to remove myself from this privileged spot. ... The prelude to my solemn and definitive expulsion. ... Why such honors bestowed on my sister, and why such hurts to me, her younger brother, born of the same mother?

The Carabinieri had escorted Frederick and his mother out of Venice many years before this, when they had descended upon the Pisani in an attempt to extort money from them. Now he was again removed by force from Vescovana, literally dragged away in chains, wrote Frederick. At one point after expulsion from Vescovana, he was traveling by train between Florence to Udine, when (so he claimed) the Italians tried to enlist him in their war against the French. When he refused,

> ... the Italians handcuffed me and put a chain around my neck; they left me with nothing but the shirt on my back ... At Milan they took me from the lock-up to the station, with a chain round my neck, at the head of a long line of scoundrels and ruffians. I still get the shivers at the thought of it.

Within weeks of that well-publicized visit to Vescovana by the Empress Frederick and her daughters, Evelina's brother published a pamphlet, *Chasse à l'homme*, in which he insulted both Evelina and the Empress. Sounding ever more like a madman, Frederick wrote:

> It ought to be known that Contessa Pisani (my sister of the same womb) is no less than the master-mind of the Triple Alliance (feminine section) and that all her efforts aim at turning it into a Quadruple alliance by the adherence of England.
>
> In fact, this woman holds in her hands the hidden strings which link Berlin, London and Rome; and this, because of the intimacy which exists

between her and H.H. the Empress Frederick. This intimacy dates from the
time when la Victoria [Empress Frederick] and la Pisani did their political
apprenticeship under Lord Beaconsfield [Benjamin Disraeli]. ...

La Pisani knew to a nicety how to exploit her master's dream. She had
everything: honours, influence and riches, whilst la Victoria had only cruel
disappointments. ... The two friends remained inseparable; they visit
one another, postmen arrive one after another at Vescovana (my sister's
mansion), their correspondence would leave diplomats of the stronger (but
so stupid!) sex looking silly.[1]

In this diatribe, Frederick presumably refers to the Triple Alliance of 1882
linking Germany, Austria-Hungary, and Italy. Part of his quarrel was also with
the British and, given Frederick's blatant anti-Semitism, Benjamin Disraeli,
the former Prime Minister who had died in 1881.

Frederick's cruelest words were reserved for his sister Evelina.

This devout countess plays around with the Jesuits, on the one hand, and
on the other, has fun and games with the Jews and the Bibliophiles [book
dealers], the veritable jailors of the pope. ...

Evelina having accepted bastardy and having besides made common
cause with all the infamies of English politics (even to the assassination of
her own mother) deserved a place near the throne.

The sting of Frederick's words did not fade with time. Six months after the
Empress's visit, Evelina's social life at Vescovana was continuing as usual. On
the occasion of her birthday on April 4, 1891, the Layards and Horatio Brown
arrived for a visit that was expected to be merry, with "joking & laughing."
But Evelina was still disturbed by her brother's unexpected and threatening
reappearance at Vescovana the previous September, and by having him seized
by the police for expulsion from Italy, this time definitively.

Early on the morning following her arrival, Lady Layard slipped alone into
Evelina's bedroom to bid her happy birthday, only to find her hostess still in
bed, and, most unexpectedly, in tears. To her old friend, a weeping Evelina
confided her despair, not only at her brother Frederick's misbehavior on the
occasion of the Empress's visit, but also his continuing "persecution" of her.
Evelina also told Lady Layard how hurt she had been by the bizarre behavior
of their late mother, Marionca. From Lady Layard's diary:

It being our hostess' birthday (her 60th) we did all we could to make it bright
for her. She admitted me into her room before she got up & I found her bed
heaped with letters & papers. She had many kind letters & a beautiful piece
of poetry from Mr Symonds & a nice one from Mr Brown.

I gave her a copy of my good old friend G[eorge] Herberts' poems—&
a doz. plants of carnations I had got from Genoa for her. We had a long
intimate talk in the course of which she sobbed bitterly at the sad thought
of the persecution she endures from her own brother & how she had been
smitten by her own mother & brother's bad conduct—but then she became
calm & brightened & I left her to dress.

If reading her brother's crazed ramblings in the pamphlet *Chasse* had left
Evelina distraught, how could it have been otherwise? But, as Lady Layard
said, after her tears, Evelina brightened. By mid-afternoon all seemed well: the
guests performed a *tableaux vivant* in her honor, and, at dinner, Don Antonio
read a poem he had written in English to celebrate Evelina, "which gave rise
to much merriment," Lady Layard recorded.

After *Chasse*, Frederick would publish six more books, including the anti-
Semitic tract, *Die Eroberung der Welt durch die Juden* (*The Conquest of the
World by the Jews*). He would die in Nice in 1901. Evelina never saw him again.

Most fortunately there was another brother—her half-brother Alexander
van Millingen, the distinguished Byzantine scholar with whom she remained
in affectionate contact throughout her life, including at Vescovana, where he
visited together with his wife. Alexander was the son of Julius's second wife
Saphiriza, and became a noted author; in 1879, he was a professor of history
at Robert College in Istanbul (subsequently Boğaziçi University), where he
remained until his death in 1915. His book *Constantinople* was published
by A & C Black in 1906 while Macmillan & Co. published his *Byzantine
Churches in Constantinople, Their History and Architecture*, in London in
1912. Her letters to Alexander show a fond Evelina: "My dearest Alex," "I
always think of you," "Your loving sister."

John Addington Symonds too remained a frequent visitor and the
closest of friends until he died in 1893. Symonds dedicated his last book,
An Introduction to the Study of Dante, to Evelina—"the Contessa Evelina
Almorò Pisani in sincere friendship and profound admiration for her noble
qualities of heart and head." Published in both the U.S. and Britain six years
after his death, it is still available. To Evelina, Symonds, moreover, had already
penned an admiring birthday poem, which he inscribed in her guest book:

To thee, O Lady, to this noble throng
you by a triple heritage belong:
Goodness and genius in your soul combine,
And beauty builds for both a worthy shrine.
By trials tempered, by the fraught of life,
By long endurance and heroic strife,
Passions subdued, and perils overpast,

you have grown yearly greater, till at last
the clear soul shining through her veil of clay....

And so on for another sixteen lines of praise for her birth, concluding with:

Feeling our heart's life in your life reborn!

After Constance Fenimore Woolson, his closest friend, apparently committed suicide in Venice in 1894, Henry James retreated in pain from the lagoon city, though not from Evelina. Here, writing from London on April 20, 1897, to Ariana Curtis in Palazzo Barbaro, James evokes Evelina in these touching words:

I bless your house and all it contains—not least the ghost of what prevails there of the presence of the noble Pisani. There ought, for her, to be no decline, but a kind of swift immersion—into the Adriatic, say, of Almorò and his Doges ... [2]

If she learned of this letter, Evelina must have been enormously gratified. But at the same time it suggests that James, that student of the independent woman, saw only a part of her personality, for Evelina was even more feistily independent than any Jamesian heroine.

It happened one summer night that a house on the Pisani estate caught fire. Evelina had rented the house to a man who drove carts around the estate. Against her advice, he had crammed into it several field worker families brought in to help with the harvest. The fire broke out in an upstairs room in which a mother had locked her three children, the youngest just three months old. Luckily, as Margaret Symonds recorded, a passing youth saw the smoke, climbed into the room and rescued the half-suffocated children, even as the house continued to burn.

A horse-drawn fire wagon arrived belatedly to try to put out the fire. The men dragged the screw mechanism of a big hose into a ditch to draw water. Then Evelina arrived. In the words of Margaret Symonds:

The Contessa descended from her barouche, and I shall never forget the extraordinary scene which ensued. With her gorgeous evening dress held up over a yet more gorgeous petticoat she swept into the crowd and addressed it collectively and individually. There was certainly a fecklessness of purpose about the proceedings, and the bailiffs issued orders which they should themselves have performed. She denounced the men, and, threatening them with a lengthy ladder which she tore from a neighbouring tree, commanded them to work.

Inspired by Evelina's words, a young man responded by jumping into the center of the burning house, dragging the hose with him. She "scrambled

after him, passionately rebuking him for his folly. She then manipulated the
syringe herself with about twenty of the natives holding up the hose behind,
the sparks flying all around, beams falling, and a general scene of glare,
confusion, pumps, and people."

The fire continued to burn until only four bare walls remained standing.

But then, as Margaret, Evelina's virtual daughter, also wrote, in her way
Evelina was a tyrant. She had to be one:

> She was a woman absolutely alone. She might have set upon a throne, for
> she had a genuine capacity for rule, and I never knew her waiver when once
> her judgement was convinced. She admitted no compromise. Some may
> have said that there was more of the tyrant than the diplomat in her but this
> was what made her great.[3]

On June 25, 1902, Evelina died after a sudden illness. It was in the midst of the
harvest season, on one of those long sunlit days when that the plaintive low cry
of the reapers recalled to Evelina the muezzins' call to prayer in Constantinople.

Alexander, the half-brother whom she loved, and who loved her, was
saddened that he had been unable to be with her at the last. "It is sad, but
there was so much loneliness and independence in her life at Vescovana that a
lonely death may seem in keeping with what went before," he wrote.[4]

On her grave is a Latin inscription written by Evelina herself. As translated
by Margaret Symonds, it reads: "Here sleeps Evelina, Countess Pisani, widow
of Almorò Pisani, whose life may be summed up in these short words, which
she herself desired should be carved here: 'Behold, I have loved justice and
hated iniquity.'"

In the London *Times* obituary notice, her father, Julius, appears
rehabilitated.

> Evelina, Countess Pisani, died on June 25th at her country residence near
> Este, in North Italy. She was the daughter of Doctor Julius van Millingen,
> the physician who attended Byron on his deathbed at Missolonghi, and who
> was known as an antiquary and an eminent medical man in Constantinople,
> where his daughter was born in 1830. She was brought up by her
> grandmother, an Englishwoman, in Rome, until she was eighteen, when she
> rejoined her father in Constantinople.
>
> About 1852 [in fact, 1853] she married Count Almoro Pisani, the head of
> the ancient Venetian family of that name, who died some fourteen years ago,
> leaving no issue. Since then Countess Pisani has managed his large estates
> in North Italy. She was a staunch friend of England and of English ideas,
> and in her beautiful home she welcomed a large circle of English friends,
> who will recall her intellectual gifts and great charm of manner. Her brother,

Alexander van Millingen, is the well-known professor of history, in the
Robert College at Constantinople.

The unsigned obituary notice fails to mention either Evelina's mother, Marionca,
or her alienated brother Frederick Millingen, aka Osman-Bey aka Major Vladimir
Andrejevich, who seems to have died in Nice, France, at some point around 1901.
Just as Marionca's *Thirty Years in the Harem* lived on, so did Frederick's crudely
anti-Semitic book *La conquête du monde par les Juifs* (The World Conquered by
the Jews). First published in French in 1874 and then in Italian in 1883 in Venice, it
was republished in Bologna in 1939, on the eve of the Second World War.

In her last will and testament, Evelina van Millingen Pisani had bequeathed
the Villa Pisani and its vast land holdings to the Marchese Carlo Guido
Bentivoglio d'Aragona, a nephew of Almorò. The Marchese had no sons, but
had a daughter who married Count Filippo Nani Mocenigo, scion of an equally
ancient Venetian patrician family and, like Almorò, a descendant of a doge.

Life on what had become the Mocenigo estate was not always easy. On
September 8, 1943, the Veneto region became a part of Mussolini's puppet
government called the Italian Social Republic, occupied by Nazi Germany.
During the Second World War the territory became a bitter battlefield, and at
one point the house, which was occupied by the Germans, was bombed. At
the end of the war, British troops billeted in the Villa Pisani found it in tragic
condition, with some of its furnishings burned in the fields of the estate.

After three generations of Mocenigo ownership, the estate was ceded to
Mario Bolognesi Scalabrin and his wife, Mariella, in the late 1960s. It was
they who carried on the work of the Mocenigos in restoring the estate to its
original splendor.

Today, the widowed Mariella Bolognesi Scalabrin continues to own and
to manage the estate with verve and imagination. The house is now an
upmarket bed and breakfast, and venue for weddings and for special events:
conferences, concerts, theatrical performances, receptions, cooking courses,
lessons in flower arrangement for the Christmas table, and other special
moments. The estate is now known as Villa Pisani Bolognesi Scalabrin.

An annual October garden show, Giardinity, is held in the carefully tended
garden of Evelina's creation. During the garden show, lectures are offered on
Evelina's exotic life and no less exotic garden. At that show, Evelina also lives
on as a brand name for tulip bulbs.

In the late 1990s, thieves broke into the chapel and vandalized Evelina's
tomb, presumably in search of jewelry. There was none: deeply religious
at the end of her life, Evelina had been buried in a simple black gown and
holding a plain crucifix.

As in the famous poem *Tulips* by Sylvia Plath, in the sleeping winter of life,
one learns peacefulness, and only the tulips appear excitable.

Bibliography

"Almanacco 1883." Trento Province. http://www.sistemazionemontana.provincia.tn.it/documenti/attach/ALLUVIONE_1882.pdf

Balfour, John, ed., *Extracts, The Van Millingen Family Papers and Writings* (1970)

Bernardello, Adolfo. "Venezia 1830–1866. Iniziative economiche, accumulazione e investimenti di capitale." *Il Risorgimento*, No 1, 2002.

Bruno, Francesco. "Last Moments of Lord Byron." *The Examiner*, No. 864 (London)

"Crede Byron, Byron and Newstead Abbey." www.praxxis.co.uk/credebyronrdeathof.htm.

Fraistat, Neil, and Jones, Steven E., ed. "The Byron Chronology." Romantic Cirlces, University of Maryland. https://www.rc.umd.edu/reference/chronologies/byronchronology/index.html.

Hsu-Ming Teo, "Orientalism and mass market romance novels in the twentieth century." In *Edward Said: The Legacy of a Public Intellectual* by Ned Corthoys and Debjani Ganguly (Melbourne, Australia: MUP Academic Monographs, 2007)

James, Henry, *Letters from the Palazzo Barbaro* (London: Pushkin Press, 1998)

Liddell, Robert, *Byzantium and Istanbul* (London: Jonathan Cape, 1956)

MacCarthy, Fiona, *Byron, Life and Legend* (London: John Murray, 2002)

Marcus, Steven, *The Other Victorians: a study of Sexuality and Pornography in mid-nineteenth-Century England* (Piscataway, NJ: Transaction Publishers, 2008)

Melek-Hanum Kibrizli-Mehmet Pasha (born as Marie Dejean or Marionca), *Thirty Years in the Harem*, Vol. 1 (Boston: Elibron Classics, Adamant Media, 2005). Facsimile of edition published by A. Ascher & Co., Berlin, 1872

Millingen, Edwin Van, *The Autobiography of a Nonagenarian*, Ch. 1, p. 4. Van Millingen family archives (unpublished)

Millingen, Julius, "Memoirs of the Affairs of Greece," *The London Literary Gazette*, No. 726 (London), Dec. 18, 1830.

Montagu, Lady Mary Wortley, *The Travel Letters* (London: Jonathan Cape, 1956)

Penzer, N.M., *The Harem* (London: Spring Books, 1965, first published 1936)

Piccolo, Maria Elisabetta, "L'Eclettismo della 'Fattoria del Doge' ovvero il parco di Villa Pisani a Vescovana." Graduate thesis, University of Venice, 2001.

Saltzman, Cynthia, *Old Masters, New World: America's Raid on Europe's Great Pictures* (New York: Penguin, 2008)

Saunders, Thomas Bailey, in *Dictionary of National Biography,* Vol. 37 (Oxford: Oxford University Press, 1903)

Smith, Albert, *A Month at Constantinople* (London: David Bogue, 1850)

Symonds, Margaret, *Days Spent on a Doge's Farm* (New York: Century, 1908)

Trenery, Gordon, *The City of the Crescent: With Pictures of Harem Life; or the Turks in 1854* (London: Skeet, 1855)

White, Charles, *Three Years in Constantinople: Or, Domestic Manners of the Turks in 1844,* Vol. 3 (London: Frederick Shoberl, Jr., 1846)

Endnotes

Chapter 1

1 Maria Elisabetta Piccolo, "L'Eclettismo della 'Fattoria del Doge' ovvero il parco di Villa Pisani a Vescovana," Ch. 1, graduate thesis, University of Venice, 2001. Ch 3, 2

2 For flood details in the "Almanacco 1883," see the Trento Province website: http://www.sistemazionemontana.provincia.tn.it/documenti/attach/ALLUVIONE_1882.pdf

3 Ibid.

4 John Davies Mereweather's interesting website is: http://www.mereweather.net/

5 See: http://www.ventaglio90.it/articolo.php?id=922

Chapter 2

1 John Balfour, ed., *Extracts, The Van Van Millingen Family Papers and Writings*, 1970, 10

2 Thomas Bailey Saunders, in *Dictionary of National Biography*, Vol. 37. (London: 1903)

3 Neil Fraistat, Steven E. Jones, ed., *Romantic Circles,* University of Maryland. For a full chronology of Byron in Greece see: http://www.rc.umd.edu/reference/chronologies/byronchronology/1823.html

4 David Laven, of *Venice and the Cultural Imagination*: 'This Strange Dream Upon the Water,"' ed. Michael O'Neill, Mark Sandy, Sarah Wootton (London: Pickering and Chatto, 2012), see: http://www.history.ac.uk/reviews/review/1282

5 George Noel Gordon Byron, Thomas Moore, Walter Scott, George Crabbe, *The Life, Letters and Journals of Lord Byron* (London: John Murray, 1860) 608

6 The Byron Chronology, *op. cit.*

7 Casey A. Wood, *Annals of Medical History*, No. 3 (London: May 1,929), 263

8 Julius van Millingen, "Memoirs of the Affairs of Greece," *The London Literary Gazette,* No. 726, London, Dec. 18

9 David Cameron Hall, *Oxford Dictionary of National Biography* (Oxford: Oxford University Press, 2004)

10 Hall, *op. cit.*

11 Francesco Bruno, "Last Moments of Lord Byron" (London: *The Examiner* No. 864, 22 Aug. 1824)

12 Julius Van Van Millingen, *Memoirs of the Affairs of Greece* (London: John Rodwell, 1831), 323

13 Ibid., 335

14 David Hill Radcliffe, "Edward John Trelawny: Recollections of the Last Days of Shelley and Byron," *Lord Byron and his Times*, see: http://lordbyron.cath.lib.vt.edu/contents.php?doc=EdTrela.1858.Contents

15 In http://en.wikipedia.org/wiki/Edward_John_Trelawny#CITEREFSt_Clair1977, citing William St Clair, *Trelawny, The Incurable Romancer* (New York: Vanguard, 1977), p. 235

16 J. Edward Trelawny, letter from Florence dated Jan. 20, 1831. *Literary Gazette* (London, Feb. 12, 1831)

17 Melek-Hanum Kibrizli-Mehmet Pasha (born as Marie Dejean or "Marionca"), *Thirty Years in the Harem,* Vol. 1. (Boston: Elibron Classics, Adamant Media, 2005), 10-11. Facsimile of edition published by A. Ascher & Co., Berlin, 1872

Chapter 3

1 Melek-Hanum (aka Marionca van Millingen), *Thirty Years in the Harem, or the Autobiography of Melek-Hanum Wife of H.H. Kibrizli-Mehemet Pasha* (Berlin: Elibron Classics, 2005), 13. Marionca's son Frederick has occasionally been cited as its author, but it is likely that she dictated it to Louis Alexis Chamerovzow, a French professor and author known to have helped her with its sequel, *Six Years in Europe.* In either case it was first published in French in Paris by Ernst Leroux in 1877.

2 Palazzo Odescalchi archives were lost in a fire in 1885

3 Peter William Clayden: "Samuel Rogers and his Contemporaries," in Lord Byron and his Times, see: http://www.lordbyron.org/contents.php?doc=SaRoger.1889. Contents

4 Melek-Hanum, *op. cit.,* 13

5 Ibid., 18

6 Ibid., 19

7 Cited in the English Catholic weekly *The Tablet* under the title "Frightful Doings of the Roman Inquisition" (London: Oct. 22, 1842), 3

8 Melek-Hanum, *op. cit.,* 21, 27

9 Letter, James van Millingen to Julius van Millingen, Nov. 29, 1839. Family archives

10 *"Family Chronicle,"* unsigned, henceforth FC

11 Letter, James van Millingen to Julius van Millingen, Dec. 21, 1841. FC

12 Ibid., Letter, Foreign Office, London, April 9, 1842. FC

13 After 1870 the Collegio Romano became a public school which was attended, incidentally, for several years by my daughter

Chapter 4

1 Lady Mary Wortley Montagu, *Letters and Works* (1837), cited in Robert Liddell, *Byzantium and Istanbul* (London: Jonathan Cape, 1956), 146

2 Robert S. Nelson, Hagia Sophia, 1850-1950 (Chicago: University of Chicago Press, 2004), 75

3 Osman Bey (Frederick van Millingen), *Les Anglais en Orient* (Paris: Ernest Leroux, 1877), 217

4 From *Colonial Church Chronicle and Missionary Journal*, Vol. IV (Oct. 1850), 139-141

5 Smith, *Op. cit.,* 48

6 Charles White, *Three Years in Constantinople: Or, Domestic Manners of the Turks in 1844,* Vol. 3 (London: Frederick Shoberl, Jr., 1846), 48-49

7 Ibid., 246

8 Robert Liddell, *Byzantium and Istanbul,* (London: Jonathan Cape, 1956)

9 Emmeline Lott, *The English Governess in Egypt: Harem Life in Egypt and Constantinople* (London. R. Bentley, 1867). Full 329-page fascinating text online at: https://archive.org/stream/englishgovernes00lott

10 Gordon O. L. Gordon Trenery, *The City of the Crescent: with Pictures of Harems in 1854* (London, Skeet, 1855)

11 N. M. Penzer, *The Harem* (London: Spring Books, 1965, first published 1936), 185-186

12 Ibid., *Family Chronicle*, 5

13 Alexander van Millingen, *The Autobiography of a Nonagenarian* (unpublished), p. 5. Alexander became a noted historian.

14 Ibid. *Family Chronicle* (undated), 6

15 *op. cit.*, 6

16 Mary Roberts, *Intimate Outsiders, The Harem in Ottoman and Orientalist Art and Travel Literature* (Durham, N. Car.: Duke University Press, 2007), 89, citing Isabella Romer, *The Bird of Passage; or Flying Glimpses of Many Lands* (London: Richard Bentley, 1849)

17 Melek-Hanum, *op. cit.*, II, 186

18 Ibid., 220

19 Frederick van Millingen aka Osman Bey, *Chasse à l'Homme* (De Gandini: Nice, 1894). In the Bibliotheque Nationale, Paris

20 Melek-Hanum, *op. cit.*, II, 213

21 Lady Mary Wortley Montagu, *The Travel Letters* (London: Jonathan Cape, 1956), 146. Quoted in Robert Liddell, *Byzantium and Istanbul*, 146

22 *The Lustful Turk* can be read online.

23 Steven Marcus, *The Other Victorians: a study of Sexuality and Pornography in mid-nineteenth-Century England* (Piscataway, NJ: Transaction Publishers, 2008), 209-210

24 Hsu-Ming Teo, "Orientalism and mass market romance novels in the twentieth century," in Ned Corthoys, Debjani Ganguly, *Edward Said: The Legacy of a Public Intellectual* (Melbourne, Australia: MUP Academic Monographs, 2007), 245

25 Roberts, *op. cit.*, 93

Chapter 5

1 Margaret Symonds, *Days Spent on a Doge's Farm* (New York: Century, 1908), 14

2 See: http://veniselapartdesanges.blogspot.it/2013/06/nous-etions-faits-lun-pour-lautre.html

3 Adolphus Slade Sir., *Travels in Germany and Russia including a steam voyage by the Danube* (London, 1840), 132

4 Ibid., 48

5 Slade, *op. cit.*, 281

6 Ibid., 131, 134

7 On this topic, see: Tara Mayer, "Cultural Cross-Dressing: Posing and Performance in Orientalist Portraits," *Journal of the Royal Asiatic Society* (Third Series), 22, 2012, 281-298.

8 Source: Nani Mocenigo archive, State Archives, Venice

9 Giandomenico Romanelli, Giuseppe Gullino, *Dai Dogi agli Imperatori* (Milan: Electa, 1997), 16

10 Ibid., 16

11 Hester Lynch Thrale (formerly Mrs. Piozzi), *The Piozzi Letters: 1811-1816*, Vol. 5, 436

12 Ronald S. Cunsolo, "Venice and the Revolution of 1848-49," https://www.ohio.edu/chastain/rz/venrev.htm
13 Alvise Zorzi, *I Palazzi veneziani* (Udine: Magnus, 1989), 380
14 Thrale, *op. cit.*, 438

Chapter 6

1 Bernadello, "Venezia 1830-1866, Iniziative economiche, accumulazione e investimenti di capitale," *Il Risorgimento*, 1, 2002 (Venice: Istituto Veneto di Scienze, Lettere ed Arti, 1996), 20. Among his other works is *La Prima ferrovia fra Venezia e Milano. Storia della Venezia Imperial regia privilegiata strada ferrata Ferdinandea Lombardo-Veneti (1835-1852)*.
2 Ibid., 20
3 Ibid., 6
4 Ibid., 5
5 Piccolo, *op. cit.*, in Ch 1
6 Piccolo, *op. cit.*, in Ch 2
7 Piccolo, *op. cit.*, in Ch 3
8 Michelle Lovric, *Venice Tales of the City* (London: Little Brown, 2003), 286-287
9 F. Bartoccini, *Roma nell'Ottocento* (Bologna: Cappelli, 1988), 60, cited in Pierre Musitelli, "Soggiorni culturali e di piacere: Viaggiatori stranieri nell'Italia dell'Ottocento," *Memoria e Ricerca* (Milano: Franco Angeli, 46/2014), 42
10 Colin Skelly, "John Ruskin, 1819-1900: A Socialist Perpective," http://www.worldsocialism.org/spgb/socialist-standard/2000s/2000/no-1150-june-2000/john-ruskin-1819-1900-socialist-perspective. Essay published in June 2000 on the centenary of Ruskin's death
11 John Ruskin, *The Stones of Venice*, quoted in: https://www.goodreads.com/work/quotes/586459-the-stones-of-venice. Ruskin's full text is available on line through the Project Gutenberg.
12 Jock Balfour, "Extracts from van Millingen Family Papers," 1970-71, *Contessa Pisani, family background*, 3. Private paper prepared for the ninetieth birthday of Frances Balfour
13 Balfour, *op. cit.*, 23
14 Melek-Hanum, *op. cit.*, 229
15 Ibid., 237
16 Frederick Millingen, *Les Anglais en Orient*, Ch. 31, 1870, cited in Balfour, *op. cit.*, 4
17 Balfour, *op. cit.*, 12

Chapter 7

1 Percy Bysshe Shelley, *Letters: Shelley in Italy* (Oxford: Clarendon Press, 1964), 330
2 Cited in Anne Amison, *Byron-Venice, An English Milord in Europe & Italy* (London: San Marco Press, 2014), 125. The Byron quote is from the diary of his radical friend in Venice, J. C. Hobhouse.
3 Balfour, *op. cit.*, 17
4 Symonds, *op. cit.*, 146
5 Henry James, *Letters from the Palazzo Barbaro* (London: Pushkin Press, 1998), 89, edited by Rosella Mamoli Zorzi (London: Pushkin Press, 1998), 89

6 Seeley, J. R. *The Expansion of England* (Chicago: University of Chicago Press, 1971, 24, cited in Manu Lakkur, "The Torch Bearer and the Tutor, Prevalent attitude towards the Roman Empire in Imperial Britain," Spring 2006 (see: http://web.stanford.edu/group/journal/cgi-bin/wordpress)

7 Leon Edel, "Introduction" to James, *Letters, op. cit.,* 13

8 Lou Agosta quotes these phrases from Ruskin in his "From Death in Venice to Empathy in Venice," March 10, 2015, see: http://empathyinthecontextofphilosophy.com/2015/03/10/from-death-in-venice-to-empathy-in-venice/

9 William Dean Howells, *Venetian Life,* Ch. 2, 1866, entire text available free online

10 Lyndall Gordon, *A Private Life of Henry James: Two Women and His Art* (New York: W.W. Norton & Co., 1996), Ch 1

11 Henry James, "Venice: An early impression," *Italian Hours,* 1909. The book represents four decades of his essays; this in Ch. 3 dates from 1872.

12 The manuscript is in the British Library but available online thanks to Baylor University and a generous donation from the Bob and Anna Wright Family Foundation of Vernon, Texas.

13 James McNeill Whistler, Letter #11542, Glasgow University, see: http://www.whistler.arts.gla.ac.uk/correspondence/people/biog/?bid=Bron_Mrs&initial=B

14 James, *Letters, op. cit.,* 91, Letter Henry James of March 15, 1887

15 Cited in John Julius Norwich, *Paradise of Cities: Venice in the 19th century* (New York: Viking, 2003), 170

16 James, *Letters, op. cit.,* 88, 89

17 Chong, Zorzi, Lingner, *Gondola Days, Isabella Stewart Gardener and the Barbaro Circle* (Boston: Isabella Stewart Gardner Museum, 2004), 136

18 Schultz, Bart, *Henry Sidgwick: Eye of the Universe – An Intellectual Biography* (Cambridge: Cambridge University Press, 2004), 408-409. Cited in Wikipedia.org/wiki/John Addington Symonds

19 LeMaster, Kummings, Ed, *The Routledge Encyclopedia of Walt Whitman* (New York: Routledge, 2013), 702

20 Sean Brady, "John Addington Symonds, Horatio Brown and Venice: Friendship, Gondoliers and Homosexuality," in Babini, Beccalossi, Hall, Ed., *Italian Sexualities Uncovered, 1789-1914* (London: Macmillan Palgrave, 2015), Ch. 11. Brady is also the author of *John Addington Symonds (1840-1893) and Homosexuality* (New York: Palgrave Macmillan, 2012)

21 See: https://sites.google.com/site/johnaddingtonsymonds/seanbrady

22 Horatio Brown, *Life on the Lagoons* (London: Rivingtons, 1904), 291. First published 1884

23 Brian Pullan, "Horatio Brown, John Addington Symonds and the History of Venice," in Chambers, Clough, Mallett, *War, Culture and Society in Renaissance Venice: Essays in Honour of John Hale* (1993), 219-221. See: Horatio Brown entry, Wikipedia

24 James, *Letters, op. cit.,* 178. Letter from Ariana Curtis to Mary Curtis, Nov. 8, 1885

25 John Berendt, *The City of Falling Angels* (London: Hachette, 2011), 148

26 James, *Letters, op. cit.,* 45

27 Marina Zorzi, "The Palazzo Barbaro before the Curtises," in Chong, Zorzi, Lingner, 191

28 Chong, ibid., 19

29 James, *Letters, op. cit.* 163. Letter to Alvin Langdon Coburn, Dec. 6, 1906

30 McCauley, in Chong *op. cit.,* 19

31 Margaret Symonds, *Days Spent on a Doge's Farm* (New York, The Century Co., 1908), 36. Preface to the second edition.

32 Curtis diary, after Oct. 19, 1888, 51
33 Cynthia Saltzman, *Old Masters, New World: America's Raid on Europe's Great Pictures* (New York: Penguin, 2008), 55
34 Rosella Mamoli Zorzi, *Un Diario 'Veneziano'*, citing letter from R. W. Curtis to Isabella Stewart Gardner, archives, Isabella Stewart Gardner Museum.
35 Henry James, *Italian Hours* (New York: Ecco Press, 1987), 1. First published Boston: Houghton, Mifflin, 1909. First published as "Venice," The Century Magazine, Nov. 1882
36 James, *Hours, op. cit.*, 2
37 James, ibid., 3
38 James, *Letters, op. cit.*, 99
39 Norwich, *op. cit.*, 169
40 Chong, *op. cit.*, 70
41 Leon Edel, *Henry James: A Biography 1953-1972* (New York, 1974, Vol I) 134. Edel worked 20 years on his 5-volume biography.
42 For a fascinating analysis of Minnie Temple and Constance Woolson, see Lyndall Gordon's *A Private Life of Henry James: Two Women and His Art* (New York: W.W. Norton & Co., 1999)
43 Brooke Allen, "Borrowed Lives," *New York Times*, May 16, 1999. Review of Lyndall Gordon's *A Private Life of Henry James: Two Women and His Art* (New York: W. W. Norton & Co., 1999)
44 Allen, *op. cit.*

Chapter 8

1 Thesis, Ch. 4, 8
2 Curtis diary, Nov. 26, 1886
3 Margaret Symonds, *Days Spent on a Doge's Farm* (New York: The Century Co., 1908), 18.
4 Ibid., 13
5 Ibid., 15
6 This account is from Compagnia del Giardinaggio, a gardening forum, and is signed by "Luca," March 6, 2014, see: http://www.compagniadelgiardinaggio.it/phpBB3/viewtopic.php?f=3&t=35186 - p3725927
7 Symonds, *op. cit.*, 20
8 Ibid., 20
9 James, *Letters, op. cit.*, 191

Chapter 9

1 Osman Bey Kibrizli-Zade', *Chasse a l'homme en pays civilise'*) (Nice: Gandini et fils, May, 1894). Kibrizli is the name Frederick Millingen used, to the point of declaring himself, at one point, Kibrizli's son.
2 James, *Letters, op. cit.*, 148
3 Symonds, *op. cit.*, 21
4 Ibid., 43